Tim Timmons

COACHING SUCCESS

Creating CHAMPIONS
for the Business World

Bristol Publishing Company
Lubbock, Texas

COACHING SUCCESS

is published by
Bristol Publishing Company

Requests for information should be addressed to:
Bristol Publishing Company, Lubbock, TX 79414-2618.
You may also visit us at our website: bristolpublish.com

ISBN: 0-9755667-1-7

Library of Congress Control Number: 2004113149

This edition printed on acid-free paper.

© 2004 by Tim Timmons. All rights reserved. No part of this book may be reproduced in any form or by any means, electronic or mechanical, including photocopying, recording, or by any information storage and retrieval system except by a reviewer who may quote brief passages in review to be printed in a magazine, newspaper or on the Web without permission in writing from the publisher.

Although the author and publishing company have made every effort to ensure the accuracy and completeness of information contained in this book, we assume no responsibility for errors, inaccuracies, omissions, or any inconsistency herein. Any slight of people, places or organizations is unintentional.

This is a work of fiction. All the characters and events portrayed in this book are either products of the author's imagination or are used fictitiously.

Printed in the United States of America.

ATTENTION UNIVERSITIES AND CLUBS: The author is available for speaking engagements. Contact him at ttimmons22@yahoo.com. Also, quantity discounts are available on bulk purchases of this book for educational, gift purposes, or as a premium for increasing charity contributions.

For my Mom.
Without her, reading would not have been fun.

Acknowledgments

There are so many people to thank in this venture. Please forgive me for rambling. First, the people who have been my direct supervisors in newspapers have taught me many things over nearly 25 years. In chronological order, thank you to Debbie Smith, Chuck Crumbo, Gail Hamilton (who passed away before this book was published), Keith Briscoe, Olaf Frandsen, Bob Lyons, Mike and Ed Meade, Jon Segal, Tom Mullen, Steve Buckley, David Ray and Charles Pittman.

I also want to thank all the people I've worked with. These people have lived through a zillion crazy ideas and my mistakes with tremendous patience and open minds. Special thanks goes to Don Bush, David Camp, Pat Cline, Shawn Everett, Ed Henry, Anna Hobbs, Richy Huneycutt, Tom Jones, Ted Jordan, Rob Langrell, Barry Lewis, Thomas Monigan, Anita Nalley, Jeri Norris, Tina Palleson, Gene Powell Jr., Chris Record, Genny Ruddick, Kevin Shaw, Carol Smith, Bob Scott, Davey Stoneberg, Lynn Sutherland, Gary Tanner, Madison Taylor, Michele Terry, Paul Trap, Patricia Robertson, Barbie Jo Walters, Alberta White, Marlene White, Jeff Wilson and Patti Young. Also Bill Winfrey who passed away in 2004.

There are also a group of folks who have offered wisdom, guidance and friendship along the way that

Tim Timmons

surely contributed much to the contents. Thanks to Mark Adams, Whitney Allman, Gerald Armstrong, Bill Bailey, Deb Bateman, Don Bolden, Jeff Brown, John Bussian, Richard Clark, Jane Emerson, Charlie Farrell, Jack Finster, Debbie Geissler, Thurman Gill, Herb Gilroy, Trip Hatley, the Rev. Michael Heintz, Mary Anne Jordan, Susan Kline, Jennie Lambert, John Lavine (and everyone at the Media Management Center at Northwestern University), Dave McChesney, Dave McCumber, Cyndi Miller, Ray Moscowitz, Brian and Joanne Norton, Tim O'Donnell, Jim Potts, Kirk Puckett, Bob Poynter, Billy Shepherd, Ken Spoor, David Stamps, Dave Sutton, Dave Taylor, Rexanne Ude, Dr. Walt Warren, Dick Wolfsie, Tom and Frances Woody and Bob and Sue Wyne.

A great deal of thanks for this particular book has to go to coaches who I've been lucky enough to have either spent a little time with or had a chance to observe. Tops on the list is Rich Clouse and then followed in alphabetical order by Jim Balsley, Terry Bartell, Dave Boggs, Brian Bowerman, Greg Carlson, Ed Clifton, Gary Gaines, Charley German, Dennis Helms, Ron Henricks, Steve House, Steve Macy, Jack McKeon, J.D. Minch, Stan Parrish, Gail Pebworth, Mac Petty, Dwayne Rater, Kevin Roy, Anita Rupar, Rick Schavietello, Mike Sorrell, Chuck Streetman, Ed Stuffle, Jerry Tarkanian, Bruce Whitehead, John Wilkins and Steve and Dave Williamson.

I also want to thank long-time friend and a guy who somehow turned my weekly sports column into something passable for the best newspaper in West Texas, Ken Brodnax. It was actually his suggestion that turned a rambling, never-ending project into what you have in your hands now. Thanks also goes to Darleen and Lee at Bristol Publishing. They have been wonderful to work with and have made my first attempt at a book a breeze. My agent, friend and partner-in-crime Dan Taylor has also been a huge influence. The title of this book was actually his idea. He has offered opinions and help in places where it was much needed and wanted.

From a family perspective, the book is dedicated to my mother who passed away a few short years ago. Kay Timmons began taking me to the library before I think I could even walk. Reading became a true joy and a passion thanks to her. My father Earl Timmons was the best man in my wedding and remains the best man I know today. My godfather Walt Smith also deserves a big nod. Not only did he allow me to use his name as the owner of the company in this story, but he taught me valuable lessons about how to be successful in life. I could not mention family without thanking my wife Linda and daughters Cassie and Cailee who have shown more patience and love than I deserve.

Thank you to Wabash College for so graciously allowing me to use its football stadium on the cover. I spent several years covering the Little Giants and have great memories of Wabash and Crawfordsville. Wabash Always Fights!

There are so many others who could easily be named here and I apologize to anyone left out.

In writing this book, the focus is primarily on the internal aspects of managing people. Although I strongly believe that nothing is more important than customer service, I wanted this effort to center on the subject of leadership and management. I tried to show the triumphs and tragedies that often occur during our working lives. I would readily admit that most of the mistakes illustrated herein are my own. Most of the things that come across as positives or successes are things I have been lucky enough to observe from others.

Finally, thank you for picking up this book. At the end of the day, it's your judgment and opinion that weigh in with the ultimate measurement — which is as it should be.

God Bless,
Tim Timmons

Chapter

1

As the seconds ticked off the scoreboard, the 5,000-plus fans on the home side of the stadium screamed in delight. Their beloved University of Indiana Huskies were about to win another championship. The clock was ticking down from :22 on the scoreboard with the Huskies up by 24. Even though this would mark the sixth time in the past 10 years U of I finished on top, the fans still loved it. In fact, they loved it almost as much as they loved the man who turned a small college from a football doormat into a perennial power.

T.J. Murphy came to Indiana a little over a decade ago and the Huskies haven't looked back since. When Murphy and his family drove into Noblesville, the football field – it couldn't really be called a stadium at that point – was a shambles. The bleachers were wood and looked like they hadn't been painted since Knute Rockne's time. The goalposts were the old "H" style and were probably being held up by rust more than anything resembling metal. The locker room was dark and dingy. It felt more like a dungeon than an athletic facility. There wasn't a single redeeming factor in the whole place, yet Murphy was all smiles as the athletic director showed him around.

"Haven't had a winning season in . . . well, it's been a

COACHING SUCCESS

while," the gray-haired A.D. had said. His name was Max Petry, but everyone on campus just called him Coach.

It actually took Max a while to figure out not only why Murphy was here, but why he was smiling. It didn't add up. Murphy was in the prime of a successful career. His teams not only won consistently, but his players went to class and graduated on time. There really wasn't any way that little U of I could attract a coach of his caliber, yet here he was . . . and he was smiling!

"Coach Petry," Murphy had said, "if you and the president want me, I think we might just be able to do something about getting one of those winning seasons."

And that had been the beginning. Sure, the first year or two were a bit rough around the edges, but there was no question that progress was being made. And it wasn't just measured in wins and losses.

Murphy had organized — or better to say had re-organized — the boosters. Within his first month, they were all out there on a Saturday morning, mowing, trimming, sanding, painting and in general working up a storm. Max couldn't quite figure it out. Normally all the boosters wanted to do was complain, but after just one speech at one of the pigskin dinners Murphy had them lined up and ready to go to work. Murphy hated getting up in front of a crowd, but learned early on that it was a skill he had to master if he was going to be a head coach. So, in Murphy's world that

> **MURPH'S PLAYBOOK**
>
> *In order to be successful, the coach has to have a vision. Wayne Gretzky calls it skating to where the puck will be instead of where it is. Coaches who win can "see" the end result long before it occurs. In this case, Murphy could see something others before had not.*

meant practice. It only made sense to the coach that when he wanted a player to acquire a new set of skills that the coaching staff had to first teach the player the skills and then practice them over and over and over. That's exactly what Murphy did on overcoming his deficiency. He took a course on public speaking and then spent hours in front of the mirror practicing. One of the first things he learned was an old lesson: Utilize what he enjoyed and was good at. He certainly enjoyed teaching and coaching, so that's exactly what he did whenever he had to give a speech.

For example, when speaking to a civic club, there would usually be several of the local high school players in the crowd. A quiet inquiry would give him the name of the one who was the BMOC, or big man on campus. By either getting to the site early, or enlisting a little help, Murphy would set the stage for what was to come later.

"Say, I hear that Scott Landis is in the crowd tonight, is that right?" Murphy would ask the assembled crowd, knowing full well the answer. "Well Mr. Landis, I hear you're a mighty fine football player, is that right?" Murphy would begin as a few chuckles rattled around the room. "Stand up, Mr. Landis, would you please?"

Then, with a nervous, but usually confident young man standing with hands stuffed inside jean pockets, Murphy would point out an empty chair on the side of the room. "Would you do me a favor, Mr. Landis," the coach would continue as curious smiles popped up here and there. "Would you walk over there to that chair?"

It might take a moment and a little encouragement, but the lanky youth would always assume his best swagger and walk to the chair.

"Now Mr. Landis, I want you to pick that chair up and look underneath it."

As the increasingly uncomfortable and now befuddled youngster looked underneath the chair, he always found a plain envelope. Puzzled, they always looked to Murphy.

COACHING SUCCESS

"Why don't you open that up and tell everyone what's inside?"

As the kid opened the envelope the eyes would always widen a bit and then in a voice that could be heard by at least those nearby, he'd say, "It's a dollar."

"Hold it up, son," Murphy would smile. "That's your dollar now. I want you to put it in your pocket and go sit down. I also want you to remember this lesson: If you want to make a buck in this life, you've got to get off your butt to do it."

The crowd would roar with delight and a young man would have a story to tell from that day forward. Murphy had seen another famous coach / teacher pull this stunt once before and thought it a valuable lesson that he could carry forward.

It was that sort of down-home country wisdom delivered with a bit of a twang that endeared the coach to the fans. Certainly he had the credentials to show that he could produce a winner, but the way he presented himself and the way he represented his school made people *want* to believe in him. Although it never ceased to amaze Murphy, understanding that principle made all the difference in the world.

That's why attendance in the Huskies Booster Club skyrocketed when Murphy got to town. That's why he was able to get all sorts of help in turning a rickety, run-down stadium into one of the finest in the country for a small school. Murphy started a fund-raiser and really got it kicked off when he held a "work day" at the stadium in his second month. Even though no one had ever heard of a workday for a stadium, Murphy wanted to send the message that the Lord helped those who helped themselves. After his first speech at a public luncheon, Murphy went to a number of boosters and told them that he'd be at the stadium on a chilly April Saturday with a toolbox, a paintbrush and some paint. If they wanted to come along, he'd grill some of his "world-famous barbecue cuisine" at the end of the day.

And what a day it turned out to be. More than 50 of the town's businessmen and businesswomen showed up in blue jeans, painter pants and all sorts of Huskies sweatshirts and jackets. By 11 a.m., most of the jackets had been shed as everyone worked up a good sweat. Around noon, runners were sent out to fast food joints to grab burgers for everyone and, true to his word, by late in the afternoon Murphy and his wife fired up six gas barbecues and grilled everyone there either a steak or a chicken breast. From seemingly out of nowhere came a few cases of all kinds of beverages. By dusk, the love affair at this small college between a football coach and a community was in full bloom.

> **MURPH'S PLAYBOOK**
>
> *It helps to add a positive twist to things. Instead of having the school's buildings and grounds crew do the work, Murph turned it into an event that helped bring the boosters together – and more importantly – put them on his side. Don't add more than necessary. Keeping things simple is still a worthy goal.*

Just as the clock ticked down to zero and the horn signaled another championship, several seniors hoisted an orange bucket overhead and dumped the icy liquid all over the spot where Murphy *had* been standing. In the flash of an eye, the 50-something coach pivoted away just as the liquid began to cascade out of the bucket. Laughing, the players grabbed their coach and threw him on their shoulders as they carried him toward the middle of the field. But before they got too far, Murphy tapped a senior captain on the head and mouthed the words, because it was too hard to hear among the celebration,

COACHING SUCCESS

"put me down." Understanding, they lowered their coach to the turf so that Murphy could greet losing coach Nick Talbot.

"You did it again, you son of a gun," Talbot said as the two old friends and rivals shook hands and then embraced. "One of these days, I'm going to be the one who's getting the congratulations instead of you."

Talbot was smiling, but only Murphy and those in the coaching fraternity could know what a tough moment this was. A year, no, a seeming lifetime of work, all boils down to a 60-minute game. Worse yet for coaches is that the game is largely out of their hands. Once the ball is kicked, the players take over – for the most part. To wind up on the losing end is a tough, tough pill to swallow.

"I know you will, Nick," Murphy said. "You're a great coach and no one deserves to be here more than you." Then he pulled his friend close and whispered "It just won't be me on the other side of the field any more . . . but don't say anything."

Before Talbot could say, ask, or even do anything else, the Huskies couldn't hold back the celebration any longer and Murphy was whisked away by the crowd. There were more hugs, handshakes and even a few tears. As Murphy got toward the tunnel, there was another large group waiting for him. This group was even more special, they were former players who came from near and far to watch their beloved Huskies and their beloved coach win another title.

Some were barely out of school and in their mid-20s. Others showed a few gray hairs here and there. To a man, they showed devotion. They all had waited respectfully off to the side, understanding that the moment belonged to the young men in uniforms now. But when their coach got to them, they couldn't hold back any longer.

So Murphy went through another round of hugs and handshakes, feeling like the guy who had just won the

Hoosier Lottery rather than just another football game. From the euphoria of winning one single game that was the culmination of months of hard work; two-a-day practices to late night and early morning (and even a couple of all night) film sessions with the assistant coaches; to the mix of emotions he felt for his coaching brother Nick; to the almost fatherly pride he felt toward his players; and now to a group of men who thought enough of Murphy and their school to come back from points near and far; especially knowing that this would be the last time he'd ever experience anything like this . . . it was the most emotional he had ever felt in his professional life.

By the time they all reached the locker room, Murphy knew what he wanted to say. As the din began to subside and the assistants hollered for quiet, Murphy stood up on top of a bench.

"Men, look around you and remember this moment. Look in the faces of your teammates. Look at your coaches. Look at your lockers, this room and look at those former Huskies who came back for this game to support you. Look hard, men, because I want you to remember this moment. I want you to be able to close your eyes 20 years from now and remember exactly what this feels like.

"This is your moment, men. You've sacrificed. You've worked hard. You've sweated. You've busted your butts. You pushed yourselves. You pushed each other. You supported each other and you never gave up.

"Teddy Roosevelt once said that the credit belongs to the man who is in the arena, whose face is marred by dust and sweat and blood. Who knows the great devotion and sacrifice it takes to get here and who are those cold and timid souls knowing neither victory nor defeat. Men, today and forevermore you know victory. You are champions, and I'm proud to be your coach!"

And with that, the players and those assembled rose

COACHING SUCCESS

as one in a great cheer. Knowing what was coming, it became too much and Murphy felt the tears flow down his face.

Early the next morning, Murphy called his old friend, the athletic director.

"Max, do you have a little time this morning" Murphy asked. "I'd like to stop by and see you."

"Sure," Petry said to the most favorite coach he had ever hired. "Come on by, Carol would love to see you, too. How about lunch?"

"No thanks, but I'll come by for a cup of Carol's coffee, if that's OK? I'll be there around 10?"

"Great," Petry said. "See you then."

He hung the phone up and stared at it for a long time. Murphy never called him Max.

Murphy's wife touched him on the shoulder as she walked by. Even though they had been talking about this for months, she still wasn't sure if he was going to go through with it or not.

"How ya doin', hon?" she asked.

Murphy looked at his wife of a quarter century. He remembered when they first met and how it had been love at first sight – at least on his part. She was a second-year teacher and he was a first-year teacher and coach. They talked briefly in the teachers' lounge at least once a day. She had a real interest in football, which made her just fine in T.J.'s eyes. It was in fact, T.J.'s eyes that sold Julie on him in the first place. She told him that she saw a fire and dedication in his eyes when he talked about his players. But she saw the wonder of a little boy on Christmas morning when he asked her out on their first date. He knew he had found the woman of his dreams – and told her so on their first date. Although she didn't say so right away, she knew it too. So here they were, almost 30 years later and she knew he was about to give up something he loved nearly as much as he loved her. Although she was excited that they would finally have a lot of time together, part of her was a little scared, too.

"Okey-dokey," he smiled. "How you doing?"

"Just fine as long as you are," she said.

The drive to Max Petry's house was only 10 minutes, but today it seemed like hours. Though this wasn't even official, T.J. knew this was the first step. He parked the Jeep at the curb and got out. He looked up and down the street and thought how the scene could have come straight from a Norman Rockwell painting. Sycamore trees lined both side of the block and the houses were mostly white wood-framed homes with brick chimneys and shutters. As he walked from the curb up the sidewalk to the front door, he noticed how Max kept the grass edged along the drive and sidewalk. Murphy smiled. He wouldn't expect anything less. Before he even had a chance to ring the doorbell, Max had thrown open the door and gave his friend a huge bear hug.

"Heck of a game yesterday, coach. That might be the best team you've ever fielded here," Petty smiled as he pulled Murphy through the door and toward the den.

"Thanks, Coach," Murphy said. "They did look good, didn't they?"

"*Look* good?" Petty exclaimed. "They *were* good. Shoot, they were great. I'm not sure they couldn't play right up there with the Boilers and the Irish."

"Whoa, let's not get carried away," Murphy laughed. "Those teams are in a whole different world than us."

"So, what brings my favorite coach calling on me this morning – considering in all the years I've known you you've never once asked to come by at 10 on a Sunday morning."

"Max," Murphy began as they walked toward the den. "It's time to hang up my whistle."

The news made the front page of the local newspaper, the Daily Herald. Normally sports stories were

COACHING SUCCESS

relegated to the front of the B section, but there T.J. Murphy was being carried off the field with a banner headline that exclaimed: Murphy Leads Huskies to Title; Retires. There were several stories; some on the game, but most on the reaction from players, fans, alumni and faculty on Murphy's surprise announcement. No one, with the lone exception of Julie, saw it coming.

Although he should've known better, Murphy was surprised that such a fuss was being made of the whole thing. After all, he was just a coach. A football coach. But to the community at large, he was an icon, a rallying point. He was the reason Saturdays were events – from tailgate parties to victory celebrations. Simply put, Murphy saw this as a natural progression. He had done the job he came to do, and although he still enjoyed the job, the time had come to move along. Most importantly, he wanted to let someone else have a chance. Sports and coaching were realms of the young – or at least not the old. And with each passing season, Murphy felt a little older.

So here he was, Monday morning at the office. It was pretty much like any other Monday morning except this time he was beginning a task he really wasn't looking forward to. He was cleaning out the office. There were boxes everywhere. Pictures with other coaches, players, school presidents, pro coaches and players. Plaques and certificates. A career all bundled up in a few pieces of paper, wood and acrylic.

The ringing of the phone made Murphy jump.

"Football office, Murphy," he answered the same way he'd been doing for years.

"Coach? Walt Smith. I was hoping I might catch you before you got out of the office."

Murphy knew Smith reasonably well, or at least as well as he knew most of the real boosters. Walt Smith owned a local business and had been a huge Huskies fan since way before Murphy came along. The coach thought

Smith to be a good guy – hard working, honest, successful.

"Just packing some stuff up," Murphy said. "I didn't know I had accumulated so much."

"I understand," Smith said. "We're sure going to miss you out there on the sideline every Saturday. And actually, that has a little something to do with why I'm calling. Can I ask about your plans? Do you have another coaching job lined up or anything?"

"No, nothing like that, Walt," Murphy said. "I'm going to semi-retire. I honestly don't have any real plans at the moment. Julie and I've talked about a little traveling. There's been a book I've thought about trying to write for a while. I really don't have any plans set in stone yet. Why?"

"Well, just an idea. Would you be willing to meet me at my office and hear me out? Afterward, you might think I'm totally crazy and laugh. Or, it could be an hour that might make a huge difference in your retirement."

"Jeez, I don't know, Walt," Murphy said. "Could you give me a little more to go on?"

"Coach, do you remember when you talked a bunch of us into painting bleachers all day on a Saturday?"

"Sure," Murphy chuckled.

"Let's just say I'm asking for an hour of your time in return," Smith said. "Fair enough?"

"Fair enough," Murphy said, even though he felt a little uneasy. "How's tomorrow afternoon around 2?"

"Great, Coach," Smith said. "See you then."

As Murphy hung up the phone, he had to admit that he was a bit intrigued.

The next afternoon at 1:50, Coach T.J. Murphy shut the door to his car and stood in the parking lot of Smith's plant. It could have been an impressive sight, but just fell short. The visitor parking lot probably held 25 or so cars. Murphy knew the employee lot in the back would have a few hundred cars and that it was full practically 24 hours a day. The lines on the blacktop were faded and nearly

COACHING SUCCESS

gone. Weeds grew in a few cracks here and there. The grassy area by the front entrance had a flagpole that reminded Murphy of the goalpost at Huskies Stadium when he arrived. The grass needed cut – badly. All said though, it wasn't remarkably different than many other plants around Noblesville. Still though, knowing Walt Smith ran this place caused Murphy to feel a little surprised. He wasn't sure what he expected, but he knew this wasn't exactly it. Walking up the sidewalk, Murphy had to tug a little harder than he thought on a glass door that was heavy and dirty. Another surprise.

Once inside, Murphy found a reception area with worn carpet, a scraped up metal desk and no one in sight. He looked at his watch and saw it was 1:55. Five minutes to spare, but it wouldn't matter if no one knew he was there.

Just then, a side door opened and a woman walked through, gave Murphy a quick glance and sat down in a huff. Picking up a nail file, she stared at a half red, half unpainted nail and, without even looking up, said, "Can I help you?" The tone left no doubt in Murphy's mind that helping him wasn't real high on her priority list.

"I'm T.J. Murphy and I have a 2 o'clock appointment to see Mr. Smith," Murphy said politely, sure that Walt Smith's name would at least get him a little attention.

He was wrong.

Punching a button on a board that Murphy couldn't see, the woman announced to apparent thin air, "Would you tell Mr. Smith that a Murphy guy is here to see him?" Then, without skipping a beat – and without looking up – she pointed to her left and said "Have a seat over there. He'll be up in a little bit."

Murphy smiled a little as he walked to a plastic chair that looked like it belonged in a cafeteria – from the 1950's. The chair had scuffmarks and smudges dotted all over it. Although Murphy was used to taking a knee in a grassy field and certainly wasn't concerned with getting dirty, he decided to remain standing. At least he was in the process of making that decision when a door behind him opened and Murphy turned to see a smiling Walt Smith.

"Coach!" Smith smiled, extending his hand. "I can't tell you how much I appreciate you coming over."

> **MURPH'S PLAYBOOK**
>
> *First impressions do matter.*

"My pleasure, Walt," Murphy said. "I've got to admit, you've piqued my curiosity a little bit."

"Good, good," Smith smiled. "That was the idea. Come on back to my office and let's talk."

Smith opened the door and Murphy headed toward it. He couldn't help but notice the look he was getting from the receptionist. It wasn't a bad look, although he wouldn't say it was a look he expected out of a professional receptionist. It was more puzzled than anything.

As the door closed behind them, they were in a long hallway with plain, carpeted floors and pictures on the walls. At the end of the hallway, a door opened into a large office that had much nicer carpet, rich wood paneling on the walls and a massive desk with a couple of plush wingback chairs in front. Smith gestured to one and waited for Murphy to take a seat.

"Could I get you anything, Coach? Coffee, tea, pop, water?"

"A cup of coffee would be great, Walt," Murphy said.

Smith walked over to an L-shaped area of the office where he apparently had a coffee maker.

"How would you like it, Coach?"

"Just black, thanks," Murphy said. He had to admit that the more time that went by the more his curiosity was getting to him. And never being the kind of guy who preferred waiting, he said, "So what's this all about, Walt?"

Smith smiled as he walked across the room with a large steaming mug in his hand. Handing it to Murphy,

COACHING SUCCESS

he surprised Murphy by sitting in the other wingback instead of going behind the desk.

"Well Coach, before I go into the whole explanation, I'd like to ask you one more favor."

Although Murphy thought he was probably a bit more patient than most football coaches, this was beginning to get a little old. Still, he did what he usually did in situations like this. He smiled and nodded. Since he really didn't know where all this was leading he believed he would learn more with two open ears than one open mouth.

"Thanks, Coach," Smith began. "I only ask that you hear me all the way out before you say anything. I *hope* that when I'm completely done that you might even hold off on any answer at least overnight. But we'll see when we get there.

"Coach, I've watched you and your teams since you came to town. If somebody would've told me before you got here that this school would be winning championships – and that this town would come out in droves to support the team . . . well sir, I would've told them that they were nuts.

"But you did it. You completely turned that school and this town around. The amazing part is, you did it not only quickly, but you made it last. At first, I thought that you got some lucky breaks in recruiting. I mean remember that Brucker kid you got right after you got here? I figured that meant you got *one* good one. But that was just the beginning. You kept getting more and more good ones. And the ones who weren't blue chips got better. Your assistants got better. You improved the efficiency of the team right in front of our eyes."

Murphy smiled the way he always did at such compliments. He'd heard them before, but still wasn't all that comfortable when someone ran through them again.

"Walt, I appreciate all the nice things, but you still haven't gotten to why we're here."

"Now Coach, you promised," Smith smiled.

Tim Timmons

Reminded, Murphy muttered a "sorry" and sat back in the chair.

"Coach," Smith began. "I've watched you and a lot of coaches for a long time. I've learned lots of things. I've learned that what you do involves leadership. It involves organization. It involves setting high standards. It involves making your players better. It involves preparing to defeat opponents and challenges. It involves crisis management. It involves crucial decisions made under fire. It involves taking criticism. It involves spreading the credit around.

"Obviously, I could go on for a while," Smith smiled. "Of course, I'm preaching to the choir here, aren't I?"

Murphy shrugged.

"What you may not know, Coach, is how those traits are exactly what I look for in my company. There isn't one thing I've mentioned that we don't deal with either daily or at least monthly. And Coach, those are traits that I have a very tough time finding in the people I hire.

"Clearly, I can find someone who embodies some of those, but finding someone who consistently does all of them . . . well, it's been a challenge."

Murphy thought back for a moment. It did seem that Walt Smith was always bringing someone new around with the season tickets his company had. In fact, Murphy couldn't remember the name of the last guy Smith had introduced him to not all that long ago as his "new plant manager." All he remembered at that moment was that there had been several of them.

"I see where you're coming from, Walt," Murphy said. "But if you're thinking that you want me to come work in your plant . . . well, I've got to tell you, I'm flattered, but I just don't think I'd be interested."

"No, Coach," Smith smiled. "I don't want you to work *in* the plant, I want you to *run* the plant."

Murphy almost laughed. "Walt, I don't know the first thing about your business. I'm just a football coach. I couldn't run a business if I had to."

"First off, Coach, it's not as complicated as you think. You know the turnover problems I've had here. I've hired people in the past with the idea that I could teach them some of the skills they're missing. I figured I could teach them how to delegate better. I figured I could teach them how to manage in a crisis. But it never worked. So why couldn't, no, why *shouldn't* I hire someone who embodies all those qualities and teach him about our product?"

Murphy thought for a long moment, trying to figure out how to tell this guy the obvious.

"Because, Walt," Murphy began, "coaches have an extensive knowledge of their 'product.' In most cases, you're talking about literally *decades* of experience. Most coaches played the game when they were kids on sandlots and in backyards. Then they graduated to an organized form when they hit junior high or high school. Some even played in college. After all that – maybe 15 or 20 years, for crying out loud – they became coaches.

"Are you really suggesting that someone who's a coach could just waltz in here and do the job without knowing a great deal about how your specific business works?"

Smith smiled. "Not really, Coach. Actually, not at all. I'm not suggesting that just any coach could come in here and do this."

"Then I'm missing your point, Walt," Murphy said. "What are you getting at?"

"I think *you* could do this, Coach," Smith said. "You."

Murphy almost laughed again, but saw the look of seriousness on Smith's face and swallowed instead. "Look Walt, I appreciate the compliment and all . . . but I just couldn't run your business. I don't know the first thing about it. I wouldn't even . . ."

"Coach," Smith interrupted. "You know how to get results. You know how to prepare a team. Shoot, you know how to build a team. We've got people in finance to tell you each month what the numbers are as well as what they mean. We've got people in product development and quality control to tell you that side of it.

"What we don't have is a leader. We don't have someone to think outside the box, so to speak. We don't have someone who inspires people to get better. We don't have someone people would run through a wall for. I think you'd be great!"

Murphy really didn't even know where to start. This whole idea caught him so far off guard and was so foreign to him that he just didn't know what to say.

Smith said it for him. "Look Coach, I know this is something entirely new to you. I don't need, or really want, you to answer right now. Go home and do some thinking. Talk to your wife about it. Figure out what you don't know that you need to know. Come up with a list of questions. Let's talk some more about it.

"Coach, all I'm asking is for you to think about it. I'm not saying you owe me anything, you truly don't. I just think this is a potential opportunity and a challenge that could benefit both of us.

"Last thing I'll leave you with is this," Smith said as they were both walking toward the office door. "Look around at major companies. Do you think all the CEOs know all there is to know about the nuts and bolts of what their companies produce? They don't. What they do know is leadership. They know what it takes to win. Coach, you do, too."

"Well Jules," Murphy was saying as they sat at the dinner table that evening. "It really did surprise me. I mean, I guess I wasn't real clear on why he asked me to come over, but I sure never guessed that was it. I mean the man offered me a job. And not just a job, but the top job."

"Don't get hung up on what's not important, dear," the ever-smart wife of a coach replied. "What's important is what you think of the possibility."

COACHING SUCCESS

"Oh, that," Murphy said brushing it aside like a pesky fly. "There's nothing to it. I mean what the hell would I know about running a business? Walt's a good guy, but he must have a screw loose up there somewhere."

"Does he now?" Julie smiled. "Seems to me he has a pretty good eye for talent."

They ate in silence for a few moments.

"I wouldn't even know where to start," Murphy said. "Hmmph! I'd probably start with that snotty receptionist."

Julie Murphy knew at that very moment that her husband would at least look at this . . . whatever *this* was. She'd seen it a thousand times over the years with him. Once he started thinking tactics, he was a man on a mission. Truth to tell, Julie thought this might be a good thing. She was never convinced that her "Murph" was ready to walk away and start fishing or worse, golf – at least in her eyes.

"It would be a little bit like starting from scratch," Julie said. "You've always said that one of the most enjoyable jobs you've ever had was that first high school job. Remember that?"

"Do I?" Murphy smiled. "They wouldn't have known a winning season if it bit 'em on the butt."

"But you changed all that, didn't you?"

"Sure. Well, sort of," Murphy said. "I didn't do it by myself. We got some good assistant coaches and we got lucky when we convinced a couple of kids to come out for football who hadn't been out before."

"So how would this be all that different, TJ? Look, I know you. I can see in your eyes that this is already rummaging around in that head of yours. You just need to know that I'll support you on whatever you decide."

Murphy smiled. He didn't really think this was something that would turn into anything serious. But at that very moment, he knew he was the luckiest guy in the world.

Tim Timmons

The alarm hadn't gone off yet, but Murphy was reaching for the notepad he kept beside the bed. It was a little after 5 a.m. and his mind was racing. Even though he still didn't think this situation with Walt Smith would possibly develop into anything, he thought there would be no real harm in writing down some questions and ideas as they came up.

His first question was: How do you measure success? Murphy might not have had a lot of exposure in business, but he knew it was about money. Was that all there was to it, though? It was so easy in football, the scoreboard at the end of the game told the tale, didn't it? When Murphy got to thinking about it, he knew that was just an oversimplification. There were games his squads won and he was madder than a wet hen. There were others that they lost and he couldn't have been prouder. The bottom line wasn't just about winning and losing – at least not completely. Did business operate the same way?

The second question he wrote down was why had so many others failed? If it was like U of I, a lot of coaches failed there before Murphy came along. In fact, that was pretty much the pattern. Whenever Murphy went somewhere new, he was always rebuilding. Surely business wasn't the same way, was it? Murphy thought this was a key point to explore the next time he and Walt talked.

He jotted down some notes on getting a feel for the folks in the plant. Are they happy? Unhappy? Content? If it was like any of Murphy's teams from the past, one or two "stirrers" could upset the whole team. It was a process that never ceased to amaze Murphy. It was usually a player who was less talented than others, but who either refused to face that fact, or chose not to. The kid would be upset about playing time, or something else – it didn't matter. The story was the same every time. The kid would get as much of the team up in arms over something that amounted to next to nothing. All of a sudden, there would be a problem. By that time, Murphy or his assistants would have to deal with it and, more times than not, the kid would end up either quitting or getting booted off the team. It was a process that always left Murphy frustrated and angry. He knew that somewhere he had failed. He hated it when he failed with kids. At least this deal with Walt Smith wouldn't have that element. After all, these were adults.

Chapter 2

The smell of bacon frying and coffee perking was the first thing Murphy noticed when he woke up. He had the notepad on his chest and the pencil still in hand. Julie must have turned the alarm off and gotten up to make breakfast while Murphy fell back asleep. He awoke with a start and didn't even notice he was alone in the bed. Rolling over, he found his slippers and trudged off.

"G'morning sleepyhead," Julie smiled as Murphy kissed the top of her head on the way to the coffeepot. "Still think this Walt Smith business is nonsense?" she said with a hint of merriment. Murphy just scowled. He hadn't even got a cup of coffee poured yet and it was obvious that his wife had seen at least a few of his early-morning notes.

"You said that I should at least think it over," TJ said. "I'm just taking your advice. Besides, I woke up early and couldn't go back to sleep."

"Uh-huh," Julie smiled.

Murphy was sitting at his desk with a notepad making more notes later that morning. He had a couple of pages of random thoughts on paper. The pages all had a line down the middle with "advantages" on one side and "disadvantages" on the other. The first advantage was simply listed as "challenge." Murph loved nothing if not a challenge. Also on the left side of the ledger were things like "Not ready to retire?"

"Opportunity to master new skills," "Chance to stay involved in community," "Opportunity to improve myself." Oddly enough, Murph noticed that he hadn't written "money" down yet. Of course, he couldn't really, could he? Smith hadn't gone into any great detail about money, but Murphy just assumed it would be financially feasible. After all, he was planning on retiring. He and Julie had precious few debts and a few investments here and there provided them with a decent monthly income. Coupled with some money they had saved, and their less-than-extravagant lifestyle, money wasn't really a problem.

MURPH'S PLAYBOOK

Never be afraid to re-think a decision once it's made, especially if it doesn't "feel" right in the gut. Although Murphy and his wife had spent a great deal of time on the decision to retire, this new opportunity gave Murphy a feeling he hadn't counted on. It would be a mistake to simply dismiss it because he had already made the decision. He knew enough to believe it important to take the time to fully analyze everything. There's a fine line between analysis and paralaysis by analysis. Know where that line is.

On the opposite side, Murphy had written things like "Can't work on golf game as much," "Can't fish as much," "Jumping into complete unknown."

After a little while, it was plain that one side far outweighed the other. Picking up his notepad and sighing, Murph headed for the living room.

"Jules, what do you really think about all this nonsense," Murph asked. "I really, really need to hear another point of view."

"Is this something you want to do," she asked?

"Don't know."

"Do you trust Walt Smith?"

"I think so, at least what I know of him."

"Can you see yourself doing something eight or 10 hours a day besides coaching?"

"That's the funny part," Murphy said. "This reminds me of my first coaching job. There's a challenge here that's got me excited. On the other hand, I don't know if I'm just fooling myself and creating something in my own head so I won't be so afraid of retirement."

Later that day, Murph picked up the phone and called Smith's plant. The phone rang seven times and Murph was just about ready to hang up when it was answered. He instantly recognized the bored voice on the other end as the same receptionist from the day before.

"Could I speak to Walt Smith," Murphy said as pleasantly as possible. I'll just kill her with kindness, he thought to himself.

The sudden click to background music made Murph blink. Why, she didn't even acknowledge me before transferring the call, Murphy thought to himself. Sheesh!

"Walt Smith," the voice on the other end said – immediately making Murphy wonder how such a pleasant guy could have such a cold and distant employee answering the phone.

"Hi, Walt. T.J. Murphy. Can I come by and talk with you?"

The memo had the entire plant doing what Murph called buzzing. "Steve Trenz has left our enterprise to pursue other interests," it read. "Please join me in wishing him the best." As if that wasn't enough, the next line really had the employees talking. "There will be a plant

COACHING SUCCESS

meeting Monday morning at 8 o'clock. Please be in attendance for a major announcement."

When Monday morning rolled around, Murphy found that he had more than a few butterflies. "I haven't felt this way since I was a young coach," he told his wife before leaving the house that morning.

"I understand," she said. "And we both know that's a very good sign."

Not a lot of people recognized Murphy as he walked in the plant that morning. The snooty receptionist certainly gave no indication that she did. She just continued to look bored as she told Murphy that she didn't think Mr. Smith was in yet.

"Oh, I'm betting that he might be," Murph said pleasantly. "Why don't you give him a buzz and check for me please."

With a sigh, she pushed a button on her console. Murphy had to suppress a chuckle when her eyes popped open a bit wider when Walt Smith obviously answered his phone.

"M-M-Mr. Smith, there's a uh . . . gentleman here to see you."

As Smith came out to greet Murph, he stopped at the desk.

"Paula, I'd like you to meet someone. This is Thomas Murphy."

Paula eyed Murphy a little differently as she extended her hand. "Nice to meet you, Mr. Murphy," she said – sounding sincere, if maybe a bit apprehensive.

"Just call me 'Murph' Mrs. . . . ?"

"Griffin," she smiled. "But I'll call you Murph only if you keep it at Paula."

"Deal, Paula," Murph smiled, happy to know that there was at least some personality behind the bored exterior. "There's hope!" he thought.

A small raised platform was put together with

wooden pallets and some sheets. Although it created a small stage about four feet off the ground, it looked like exactly what it was – a makeshift something or other. On top of the contraption was a small dais with a microphone. There was also a folding metal chair.

Walt Smith approached from the side and stepped up on a large wooden box that served as a step. He walked up and turned on the mike, producing a predictable screech. He took half a step back and the screech went away. A couple of taps on the mike and an obligatory blow to ensure it was on signaled everyone that he was ready to begin.

"Thank you all for coming. While I know many of you are already scheduled to be here as part of your normal shift, many more of you are here when you would normally be sleeping or doing something else. I wouldn't ask you to take your scheduled time off and come in for a meeting – or take you away from your normal working duties for that matter either – if it weren't important.

"You all know that we've had several plant managers over the past few years. Too many. Too many for all of you. Too many for me. And most importantly, too many for our customers.

"I've heard that the definition of insanity is to do the same thing over and over and expect a different result. That's why we're here today – because we're not going to continue to do the same thing . . . or more importantly, we're not going to continue the insanity.

"In the past, we've hired plant managers. They were all given the same incentive – do a good job and we'd move them into the CEO spot so that I could retire."

Smith saw that he not only had everyone's attention but had them hanging on each word.

"One of the mistakes I've made in all this has been to only "commit" three-quarters to each plant manager. It was my thinking to let them learn to walk before asking them to run. I see now – despite my intentions being good

— that that was a mistake. I should have been looking for someone who was capable of hitting the ground running when they got here instead of hoping that they'd grow into it. That's one of the reasons we're doing it differently this time.

"What you, I and our customers all need is someone who knows how to win. We need someone who's a leader. We need someone who can not only work but thrives under pressure.

"I don't have to tell any of you about pressure. None of us have made any bonuses the past few years. You're all sick and tired of the cost-cutting measures we've had to put in place. And although I believe in the old saying that 'what you do speaks so loudly I can't hear what you're saying' I also don't think that it's just idle talk when I tell you that I believe we've finally found the person who can stop the insanity. I believe we've found the right person who can turn the fortunes of our plant around. I believe we've found the person who can help us all succeed. Ladies and gentlemen, colleagues, it is my distinct pleasure to introduce you to our new chief executive officer, Mr. Thomas Murphy."

As Murph came out from behind the door that he had been waiting behind, it struck him that although the applause wasn't "forced," it was polite at best. Even though he had been introduced at a few press conferences as a new coach, he wasn't at all sure that he ever gotten a more dubious reception.

"Good morning," Murph smiled into the microphone. "I'm truly pleased to be here today and I'm excited about the prospects we have in front of us. I'll be perfectly honest. I have very high expectations of myself and of what we are all going to do. I believe to be successful we have to plan to be successful. You'll all play an important part in that. I want you to know that my door is open and in the coming days I'll be around every department so that I can get to know all of you. At this point, I'd be pleased to take any questions."

As Murph looked over the crowd, he recognized a few of the faces. There was a former player or manager here and there. He saw a few girls he recognized from the cheer squads of years past. It was then that he noticed a couple of them were just staring with open mouths. Finally, after a long silence, one person in the crowd raised their hand.

"Could you tell us what sort of experience you have in plant operations?"

"None at all," Murph said. "My background is in coaching football."

The silence was deafening.

At 4 p.m. that afternoon, Murph had his first meeting with his senior staff. While most of the day had been spent unpacking boxes and arranging the new office, Murph had been fine-tuning the notes he was up most of the night working on. To be honest, Murph and Walt Smith had gotten exactly what they expected. Both knew that it would take some time – and more importantly – some results before anyone at the plant would embrace their new leader.

"Most of them probably figure the owner of the company ought to be taking one of his own drug tests," Smith had joked.

Murph knew that the statement wasn't that far from the truth. Murph had been around enough teams to know that getting off to a good start could help tremendously. However, you couldn't fool a whole team for very long. Good start or bad, sooner or later he would have to deliver. That's why Smith had hired him and that's what he intended to do. He also knew that his first meeting would go a long way toward determining how quickly things could get going. Which way they might go depended entirely on Murph.

"I'm telling you, he's a great guy," Matt Burgin told

COACHING SUCCESS

some of his co-workers while they were on break.

"I don't care how good of a guy he is, Matt," Cheryl Wagner said. "Being a good guy isn't the point. How in the world is he going to run this plant? He has no experience. I've got an out-of-work husband and two kids. I can't afford this company to keep screwing around with my future. This guy is just a football coach, for crying out loud."

"And he was a damn good one," Bill Russell chipped in. Bill had more than 30 years in and when he talked, others tended to listen. "But no matter how good he was, this ain't figuring out whether to punt or go for it. This is about how we're going to reach quotas – keep quality control happy – hit dock deadlines. This is about running an operation."

"I know, Bill, I know," Matt said. "But you've said yourself many times that the boss was worrying too much about the stuff they pay us to worry about. You said that we needed somebody who knew how to be a leader and who could lead this plant back to good times again. And I'm here to tell you, Coach Murphy is a leader."

The new leader of the plant walked into his first staff meeting. There were several decisions that he had already reached. First, he wasn't there to blow sunshine up anyone's pant legs. He'd know soon enough if they were going to come around or not. Walt had talked to Murph at some length about that. Walt explained to Murphy that too many new managers, from first-timers to upper-level guys, had an identity crisis. The new manager thought they had to convince everyone that he/she was the boss. This was one of those amazing facts in business that Walt said no one could figure out. When a new boss comes in, everyone already knows that person is the boss. The only one worrying about it is that person. Why he/she doesn't just walk in and start working was beyond him, Smith said. It really turns into a paradox. The more someone worries about whether or not everyone knows he/she is the boss, the less gets accomplished, so the less everyone thinks of the new boss. Eventually, if the trend doesn't reverse itself, the new boss doesn't have to worry, because he/she isn't the boss anymore. "Look at it like your football team," Walt advised. "Did you ever walk into a locker room and try to convince your players that you really were the coach? Well, I don't know why managers seem to think they have to. You're in charge. Remember that when you walk in."

Murph had also decided that he also wasn't there to evaluate anyone today or make any long-term decisions based on short-term observations. He knew that his staff would need a little time to digest everything. It wouldn't be fair to make evaluations today.

The third decision Murph had already reached was that he would do two things in this meeting. An old coach had told Murph a long time ago that on his first day with a new team he should "turn the volume up." What he meant was that a new leader couldn't walk in and try to be everyone's friend. A coach, just like a boss, can't be a buddy to everyone. Walk in and "turn up the volume," Murph remembered the coach saying. You can always turn it down later, so to speak. But you sure can't walk in with the volume turned down and then try to crank it up later. It'll never work.

So, Murph was walking in with the volume on high. He had also decided that there was no way he could do this without learning how the business worked. So, he was going to ask lots of questions. The important part of this, Murph knew, was in listening to the answers. It was just like on the football field. If a linebacker told Murph at halftime that the opponent was running a blocking scheme that negated the defense's strength, Murph knew that he should listen. The linebacker was on the field. He had likely been hit pretty hard several times and had a much better perspective than a coach on the sidelines or in a press box. Only a fool wouldn't listen to someone who had a better perspective. Murphy was many things, but a fool was not one of them. Listening was invaluable.

> **MURPH'S PLAYBOOK**
>
> *It's also important to know what you're listening to.* Murphy knew that most information from a player on the field was likely good – if *the player had a good understanding of X's and O's. If not, the information might be suspect. A good coach knows how to listen and knows what to heed and what to discard.*

The senior staff consisted of eight people. Most of them had more than 20 years with the company while a couple of them were "newcomers" at 10 years of service or less. One of the "rookies" was a woman, as was one other. Ironically, the only football fan in the bunch was Beatrice White, or just plain Bea. She had graduated from U of I and knew Murphy from her college days. It would be fair to say that she was one of the few who were even close to giving Murphy the benefit of the doubt.

Bea was by far the shining star of the team. After U of I she headed to Indianapolis and got her master's in record time. Now in her 30's, Bea was well liked and respected throughout the plant. She was still in great shape. She and her husband had what appeared to be a picture perfect marriage and were the life of all the company's social functions. Although Bea was constantly on the go and always seemed to be in something close to a controlled frenzy, her department was always on top.

The opposite of Bea was Billy Polaski, although not from a talent standpoint. Billy was very, very good. The problem was he not only knew it, he was quick to tell everyone who would take the time to listen. In some ways, Billy was a real puzzle. He certainly wasn't well liked, but he did have one of the top departments in the plant. Those outside joked often about how shallow he was, but those who worked for him performed at amazing levels and were loyal.

Dave Eads was the lone black member of the team. At 40-something, his weight was a worry to his peers who truly liked him and wished he had the discipline to not only do something about his lifestyle, but also with his staff. It was tough for Dave to handle the occasional issue that arose among workers. Therefore, accountability wasn't a big issue in Dave's department and the results showed it.

A department that showed great results was the one run by Denise Doubet. If anyone had taken a vote on who was most likely to succeed, it would've been a close race between Bea, Billy and Denise. All three were immensely talented, yet the three were about as far apart as three people could get. Denise, or Double D as her staff sometimes called her – when she wasn't around – was a climber. While that can be a good thing in some cases, Denise clearly didn't care if she stepped on someone else while she was reaching for the next rung on the ladder. So while she might win the "likely to succeed vote," she wasn't going to win any popularity contests.

The last woman on the team was 60-ish Marti Beech. If there was anyone as nice as Bea it was Marti. She also had the most seniority with a little more than 44 years. She started working at the plant straight out of high school and had been promoted by default more than anything else. She wasn't at all innovative. Problems could stop her dead in her tracks. She did follow orders well, though. That, plus a cheerful disposition and a "company" attitude helped push Marti a few notches higher than she should have gone.

Oscar Torres also moved up with the help of his attitude. The only problem with the 55-year-old was that he would say one thing and do another. Oscar always made a great first impression and could easily be the life of the party. But it wouldn't take long before he would brag himself into a corner. He never really did it maliciously. In fact, it would be fair to say that most people liked him; they just didn't respect him.

The seventh member of the team was Joseph Cox. If there were a prize for the smartest member of the senior management team Joseph would have won it hands down. An Ivy League education and an analytical outlook seemed to put Joseph on a different level than his peers. He kept himself apart even further when he talked. Within minutes, Joseph's monotone could take any excitement out of any room. It's not that he did it on purpose, he just had no rapport with his staff, his peers, his boss, anyone.

The room had an air of anticipation and the buzz-buzz of muted conversations while everyone waited on Murph to arrive. Everyone was there except the final member of the senior staff, Charles, who was second in years of service only to Marti at 42. He hadn't been on time to a meeting in years. Most of the managers believed Charles actually enjoyed coming in late and disrupting what had already started. Charles was in his early 60's and constantly talked about the old days when everyone worked hard at their jobs and appreciated what they had. It was almost comical because if there was one person in the plant who didn't work hard and especially didn't appreciate what they had, it was Charles. He was a prime example of someone who thought they should make more each year regardless of the quality of their work or productivity. To say that Charles was bitter would be an understatement. Even with all that though, his peers were surprised that he would come in late again today.

The door opened and Murph strode in, walking not in a rush but with a purpose. He walked around the long polished table and took the head seat. Murph sat his notebook down and appeared for a second to be lost in a thought. The room grew still.

> ## MURPH'S PLAYBOOK
>
> *One of the positives the senior management team had going for it was diversity. The group was a pretty good mirror to the community. Murphy had learned a long time ago that having a diverse staff was hugely important. Look at it this way, he had told a group of coaches in a clinic, if you were going to pick the best football team of all time from players past and present, who would you pick? As the coaches brought up names recognized by all, Murphy waited a little bit before asking the coaches to look at their lists and notice how racially diverse it was. It would never make sense to try and assemble the best team possible while keeping out one group or another.*

"During the next few weeks you're mostly going to hear me asking questions," Murph opened. "This morning, however, I want to open with a statement.

"Some, if not most or all of you, might be wondering why I'm here, why I was hired. You might be asking yourselves how in the world I got this job. You might be downright dubious about my qualifications.

"Well, I want to clear that part up right away. I wouldn't begin . . . "

The door opened and Charles walked in, his trademark pipe in his mouth, trailing a thick whirl of blue-gray smoke. "Sorry I'm late everybody," Charles said. "I got hung up in . . . "

"Please, have a seat," Murph interrupted in a firm, but not unfriendly voice. He then waited while Charles lingered a second longer than he should've before moving to his customary spot at the table.

"I wouldn't begin to tell you that I have any sort of experience or knowledge in any of the technical aspects of our industry," Murph said, picking up exactly where he left off without skipping a beat. "However, please don't mistake that to mean that I am not qualified or even excited to be here. I have been hired to help improve this operation and to make it profitable. And that's exactly what we're all going to do.

"You all need to know that I need and want you on this team," Murph continued as he looked around the table at each one there. "The problems that this plant faces are all of our problems. No one is in this alone. We're all in the same canoe, so to speak. If a canoe has a hole in one end, the other end has a problem as well."

He paused and smiled just a bit.

"Look, we have a great and challenging task before us and I just want to make it clear that none of us have time to spend on office politics, busy work or anything that's not helping us all reach our goals. That's going to be a big part of my job. If you have something in your way, let me know and together we'll find an answer. I can't tell you all how excited I am to be here and to be part of this team, part of your team, part of our team."

Murph smiled again. "Any questions?"

As so often happens when people are

> **MURPH'S PLAYBOOK**
>
> *One of the most important qualities for a coach in setting up a game strategy is the ability to get rid of unnecessary distractions and disruptions. A good coach can seem almost ruthless in removing roadblocks and obstacles that stand in the way of a team.*

in a new situation, no one wanted to be the first to risk saying anything, even though literally everyone in the room had things that they were intensely curious about.

"None?" Murph smiled. "That's OK, that's fine. I've got enough questions for everyone, so I'll go first.

"Why aren't we making our goals?" Murph said in a decidedly friendly voice. He had planned for this as he prepared for this meeting. Years of players sitting quietly on their hands had taught him that. Still, getting off on the right foot with straight questions and (hopefully) straight answers was the way to go, he surmised. That's why he thought the best strategy was to start out asking the tough question first in a non-threatening way.

No one said a word. Murph expected that. He waited. Finally, Dave Eads raised a hand and said, "Mr. Murphy, I think we all know that our results haven't been up to expectations. But exactly what goals have we missed?"

Of all the questions Murph anticipated, that wasn't one of them.

"I'm sorry," he asked. "Help me understand what you're asking please."

"You said goals, sir," Dave said. "As far as I'm aware, I haven't had any goals in my department." Dave had been at the plant for about 20 years and was generally regarded as a good guy, but one who could be (and was) taken advantage of by his staff.

"How did you measure your success or progress," Murph asked, not a little surprised.

"Well frankly, sir, we just didn't," Dave answered. "We were just always told to try and do better."

"But didn't you ask what that meant?"

"Questions like that weren't encouraged," Denise chipped in. "We had goals a few years ago, but that was also a couple of managers ago."

Murph was stunned. However, he believed that much like coaching it was important to not let his staff see any sort of negative reaction – unless he really wanted them to.

COACHING SUCCESS

"OK," he said, beginning to make some notes on his legal pad. Inwardly, he had his first thought of just how large the task in front of him might really be. "Here's the deal. I've been through our budget. Before the end of the week, I'd appreciate it if each one of you would create goals based on the performance levels needed to achieve budget. Then, we'll take . . ."

Oscar Torres' hand shot up. "Excuse me, Mr. Murphy. I don't know about anyone else, but I don't have a budget."

A chorus of agreement rolled across the table.

Murph nodded and made more notes. "As a coach, we had some pretty clear objectives. It might seem simplistic to say that it was just about winning, but it wasn't. We wanted to win, *and* we wanted to win the right way. We wanted to turn out winners on the football field who would learn the skills and disciplines necessary to become winners off the field as well. We had some very clear and measurable ways to gauge our progress. There were games each week. We won or we lost. There were dean's lists each semester. Our players made it or they didn't. There was graduation. Our players graduated. And then there's life after school. Our players did well."

"Or didn't," Charles muttered.

"Excuse me, I didn't catch that," Murph said.

"I said, 'or they didn't,'" Charles repeated a bit louder. "You said that *things* happened or they didn't. But when you got to the last couple of things, you left off the negative side. But that's OK. I mean it doesn't sound as good if the story doesn't end with a happy ending."

The only person at the table who wasn't surprised at the short outburst was Murph. Virtually every team he had ever coached always had at least one player who was what Murph called a stirrer. Sometimes they were talented, and much more difficult to deal with, and sometimes they weren't. But every team had at least one and Murph expected the working world to be much like his past teams.

"Actually," Murph said in his most friendly professor-type voice, "I didn't."

"Beg your pardon, sir," Charles said with a little too much emphasis on the 'sir,' "but you did leave off the part about 'they didn't.'"

"That's because they did," Murph said with as much charm as a man could muster. "I was fortunate enough that every player who stayed four years graduated and went on to do productive things in life." Without taking much of a breath, he charged forward. "But that's not why we're here, so back to the task at hand. Do I understand that none of you have departmental budgets, goals or objectives?"

Charles put his chin on his chest and crossed his arms. The rest of the staff's quiet nods told Murph what he needed to know. "By the end of tomorrow, you will each have your department's budgets and all the departmental data that I do. We'll then spend a little time going over all of it to make sure everyone understands what they've got and then we'll figure out how to share any appropriate data with our folks on the front lines."
"But we've never done that before," Billy Polaski said.

"Noted," Murph said.

"OK, I mentioned questions before. Anyone have anything yet?"

Hands all across the table shot up.

Chapter 3

When Murph pulled into the driveway that evening, he was as tired as he could ever remember being at the end of a day. "I'm getting too old for this," he thought as he climbed out of the Jeep. He thought that was a line from a movie, maybe Butch Cassidy and the Sundance Kid, one of his favorites. He also thought of a line from some other movie that said something about if you loved your job you'd never spend another day working the rest of your life. He wondered if this would end up being work or not. As he walked toward the house, he was what he called "dog-tired." Before his hand reached the doorknob, Julie opened it and was waiting on him with a smile and a cold beer!

Although Murph had planned on getting farther in the first meeting with senior staff, the outcome wasn't totally unpredictable or necessarily bad. He knew the first task was to teach his team – yes, he was already thinking of them like many other teams before – how to play to win. Right now, they were just showing up for work, going through the daily routine. He had to get them to start playing for the victory. They had to have goals. They also had to have skills – an area that concerned Murph more about himself than the rest of the team. It was, however, becoming quickly apparent that

Tim Timmons

"playing to win," just wasn't present – at least not at this place. That fact alone dazzled the football coach. How could you go to work day in and day out without trying to accomplish what it was you were getting paid to accomplish? Teaching people to play to win would be his first priority.

He knew that in this business, just like in football, it wasn't about pre-game or halftime speeches. That happened far, far fewer times than the average fan thought. No, 90 times out of 100 the team with the most skills and talent won the game. The remaining 10 could be chalked up to any number of factors, leading the way being luck of the bounce. If, as a coach, he made sure his team had superior skills, then the lucky – or unlucky – bounces usually took care of themselves.

> **MURPH'S PLAYBOOK**
>
> *"Play to win" is one of the most important points Murphy had to make. In sports, playing to win is a given. Very few participants play a game with the intention of losing. Even friendly games produce a winner. But in business, "winning" can be a fuzzy image at times. "Winning" should be defined and strived for in every appropriate way.*

And when it came to skills, he knew that was where his own personal trouble would fall. Instinctively, he could watch a lineman and see where his footwork was off or where he dropped his hands too low. He could watch a quarterback and spot right away that he was throwing off his back foot or that his follow-through was cut short and caused the ball to sail over a receiver's head. But the plant was a different story. He could stand there all day long and watch people on the front lines work and not

COACHING SUCCESS

recognize effective and ineffective techniques. That would have to change – and fast. He wasn't as worried about the managers. Management and coaching were a lot alike. At least that's what Walt Smith was banking on, he thought.

He also knew that the first senior staff meeting won him a few converts. He still had some to win, but no one won the conference in the pre-season. Right now, Murph had to build relationships, define success, teach his team how to play to win and help his squad improve their skills so they could indeed record the victory when they got in position.

He remembered one of his first booster breakfasts when the Huskies had lost. It was his second game at Indiana and they had won the first game in an upset. They almost had the second one when the quarterback fumbled and the other team scored as time ran out to win. The boosters had been pretty mad and had nearly accused Murph of fumbling the ball himself. Murph explained to the group that the Huskies won as a team and lost as a team. One play never, ever, ever won or lost a game. Without the 70 other plays, the one everyone talked about couldn't have happened. Over time, he also taught the boosters that a coach's job was to put players in position to be successful. Coaches can't tackle, run, pass, block or kick. But if they do their job, the players would improve their skills, thus enabling them to more often be in a position where they could be successful.

He knew that that basic philosophy would never be truer than in his new job.

At 7:45, Murph buzzed the intercom and his secretary Effie Perez quickly answered.

"Yes, sir."

Effie Perez had worked at the plant as executive secretary for almost 20 years. Without a doubt, Murph knew she was one of the few bright spots. He also figured that ultimately she probably was the one who really ran the place.

"Mrs. Perez, would you ask Charles to come see me when he gets in please?"

"Can't do it, boss."

"Why not?"

"Because you insist on calling me Mrs. Perez even though I've done everything except clobber you over the head in telling you to call me Effie."

"I'm sorry, Effie," Murph laughed. "If it's any consolation, I still call my wife Mrs. Murphy on occasion."

This time it was Effie's turn to laugh. "I know," she said. "She and I talked last week about you and she told me you were going to be my biggest challenge yet. However, she did tell me the secret."

"What's that?" Murph asked. But there wasn't any answer. He pushed the intercom button again and still nothing.

The door opened and in walked Effie with a cup of steaming hot coffee. "Your wife said that if I just kept you supplied with coffee that was strong and hot, everything else would take care of itself." Effie didn't add that Julie Murphy had also told her to switch Murph to decaf, a trick she had pulled herself at home a couple of months ago.

"Jeez," Murph said. "Between the two of you, what chance do I have?"

Murph got busy going through the budget packages the CFO had prepared for him and senior staff. He hoped they were spending as much time analyzing the numbers as he was. In fact, he was finding that the numbers told stories just like plays out of his old playbook. He was so absorbed that when he reached for a sip of coffee, he noticed it had gotten cold. He looked at his watch and it was 8:40. Surprised, and a bit annoyed, he pushed the intercom button again.

"Yes, boss?"

"Did you not find Charles," he asked. "I thought we were going to ask him to come in when he got to work?"

"Yes, boss," Effie said. "But it's kinda tough since he hasn't arrived at work yet."

Murph knew that senior staff came to work around 8 each day. In fact, most of them were like Murph in that they got there early. Well, "most" wasn't all.

About five minutes later, the intercom buzzed. Murph pushed the black button.

"Charles is here as you requested sir," Effie said in a much more formal and business-like tone. "Shall I bring him in?"

"That would be great, Mrs. Perez."

When Charles walked through the door, he had his pipe as usual and the usual smoke trail. It was clear from his expression that he wasn't excited to be here – although he had the good sense to hide it somewhat.

"Thanks for coming in, Charles," Murph began. "Although I expected to see you about 45 minutes ago."

"Well, yes," Charles harrumphed. "I had a flat tire on the way to work this morning."

"Those things happen," Murph said as he noticed that Charles' fingernails were as clean as could be. "But this is exactly why I wanted to see you.

"You were late for yesterday's meeting and I would just like to make sure that you understand that I'd appreciate you being here on time from now on." Murph had purposefully left out any mention of Charles' habit of always being late. After all, Murphy was only concerned about what happened from this time forward.

"Look," Charles bristled. "I suppose everyone has already told you that I am usually late to those meetings. So fine, you want to crucify me, go ahead."

"Actually," Murph began. "I'm not interested in your history. A wise man from South Carolina once told me that only two good things come from the past, lessons learned and pleasant memories. All I'm interested in is from here forward."

"Fine," Charles snapped. "I'll do my best."

"Well Charles," Murph started in a friendly voice. "Frankly I expect more than that." Murph leaned back in his chair and smiled his most disarming smile – at least he hoped it was. "You're senior staff. You're a valuable part of this team. It won't work to have people showing up at all different times. We have to respect each others schedules and be prompt."

"I said I'll do my best," Charles snapped a bit too harshly. "My best is all I can do, sir," he snapped. And with that, he headed for the door. Murph let him go ahead – almost. Right before Charles reached for the knob leading out of the office Murph softly said, "Charles, I hope we can put this awkward start we seem to have gotten off to behind us. I meant what I said about you being a valuable member of this team.

"But Charles, you need to know that I'm not going anywhere," Murph continued in a straight and level voice. "And this is going to be anything but business as usual from here on out. We're going to turn this plant around, I hope that means you and I, but that's a whole lot more up to you than it is to me."

Murph had said everything to Charles' back and that's all he saw as the door slammed loudly shut.

Murph called another meeting of senior staff to go over the budget and performance packages each had been given. This time, everyone was there on time. In fact, they were all there early and were arguing back and forth when Murphy came in.

"These numbers are impossible," Charles said.

"Mine, too," Billy chipped in.

"And mine . . ."

Murph stood at the head of the table and raised his hands. "Good," he said. "In this room with those doors shut this is exactly the kind of discussion I want to hear. Only by being totally honest with each other can we make sure we work out all the bugs.

COACHING SUCCESS

"Now, what's wrong with those numbers?"

Everyone started talking at once – everyone that is except Bea. She was uncharacteristically quiet.

Again, Murph had to raise his hands to quell the noise. "I notice you're not protesting," Murph pointed out to Bea. "So, that means you're OK with your department's numbers?"

"Depends on what you mean by 'OK,' I guess," Bea said. "We are already doing much better than anything I see in this packet."

Murph's first reaction was, well, good. At least I have one area I don't have to worry about. But then the thought struck that under-projected could be just as harmful as over- projected.

"So what do we do about that?" he asked.

"I was afraid you were going to say something like that," she answered. But there was a definite smile, Murph noticed. Good for her, he thought.

"Anyone else think their numbers are too low," Murph asked and waited. When no one said anything, "OK, so if we think the rest of these numbers are a challenge, what can we do about it?"

"Nothing," Charles said. "I mean some of these numbers that I'm looking at represent a 45 percent increase. There's no way we can possibly do that."

"It's interesting that you use the word 'possibly,'" Murph said. "Tell me, what would it take to achieve that goal if there are no limitations?"

There was a long pause as if Charles was measuring the validity of the question. "Well, I'm not sure it would make any difference. I mean we're talking about something that's never been done before."

"I understand," Murph said. "But we're talking about some work that involves speed and good hand-eye coordination – or at least we are in this case, right? If we brought in, oh I don't know, say the national table tennis team and trained them for a month, would that work?"

A few chuckles were heard around the table – at first. But one by one you could almost see the light bulbs going on. A seemingly silly comment had the senior managers seeing a possibility instead of a roadblock.

"Look folks, there must be a hundred ways to get something accomplished," Murph said. "We just have to decide on some of the best ones that will help put us in a position to succeed. We then have to make sure that every day we do that. I don't want to oversimplify it, but at the same time, I don't want to make the process too complex either. We certainly have some things in this plant that are indeed complex. But teaching people to come to work every day and do the kinds of things it takes to be successful, well, that's neither complex nor hard. It's a habit of playing to win and it's something we have to start. And we have to start today.

"I gotta tell you guys, I'm going to use an awful lot of football analogies because that's what I know. If that bothers anybody, let me apologize now. However, I don't think it's going to change and I hope you'll either bear with, or forgive me. With that said, there are some football teams who just show up and go through the motions. They go through the motions in practice and they go through the motions in games. Sure, they may win a few, but they won't win any championships. They just play. They never learn to play to win."

"But how do we do that?" Dave asked. "How do we play to win?"

"We help people get better at the critical skill sets," Murph said. "We help them get better every day. An All-American from Penn State once told me that he didn't believe people came to work every day with the intention of doing a lousy job. He's right. So all we have to do is help them get better.

"I kidded about the U.S. table tennis team, but we're talking about physical and mental skills. Those things can be improved through practice, through teaching, through nurturing.

"How many of you have any sort of ongoing training program that helps your people get a little better every day?" Murph asked.

"Wait a minute," Charles said. "Most of these people don't have time to play silly games and concentrate on that stuff. It's counterproductive. They come here to work. That other crap is just an intrusion on the real work. It impedes the real work."

"Intrusion?" Murph asked incredulously. "We want to find ways to help make people better so they can make more money. We want to help them improve so they can create their own job security. You're telling me that they'll have a problem with that? Come on folks, if that's the kind of people we have then that's a problem in itself. But I'll tell you this, the only players I ever had on my team who didn't want to get better weren't really interested in playing football. People don't come to work every day and see how little they can do or how much they can goof off.

"Our job is to continually challenge them, to engage and energize them . . . "

Murph stopped talking. Suddenly. He smiled a little and looked around the table at each of the senior staff. "I'm sorry folks," he chuckled. "My wife and my assistant coaches tell me I often launch into a speech without meaning to. I think I just did it again.

"So, back to business. Everyone have a chance to go over your numbers?" Murph asked. "While we may have some different ways of looking at it, these at least offer us a starting point."

With that, Murph reached under the table and opened a large cardboard box. Inside were three ring binders. On the covers, each one had the name of someone seated at the table. Half went to his left and the other half to the right.

"I'd be obliged if you would all keep these handy as

we move forward," Murph said. "Keep notes from our weekly meeting in there. Keep notes and ideas from your departments. Record important news and notable events.

"There may even be a few more things they can be useful for, but we'll talk about that later. For right now, please open them to the first page."

Inside, the front sheet that was already in the binder has a lined piece of paper with big, bold letters at the top. It simply said, ***"Play to Win."***

"I know we talked about this briefly already," Murph said. "Anyone have any ideas on what "play to win" means in our plant?"

"We hit our numbers," exclaimed Dave confidently.

> **MURPH'S PLAYBOOK**
>
> *Whether it's three-ring binders or something else, giving the team something they can use as guideposts can be very helpful.*

"We hit *all* our numbers," Denise corrected.

"We continually improve," offered Bea.

"How about we – at least in my department – reduce the error totals and remakes?" Marti asked.

"Gee, does this mean we'll have cheerleaders, too," Charles tossed in sarcastically.

The table went quiet. Everyone either looked intently at her or his new notebook or at Murph.

The old coach didn't skip a beat. "That depends on whether or not we post *really* big numbers, Charles," Murph smiled. "But seriously, what would a win in your area look like?"

Charles paused for a minute, but before he had a chance to respond, Bea jumped in and said, "You could improve shipping times or reduce the amount of mis-ships."

"Oh sure," Charles said with more sarcasm. "And

COACHING SUCCESS

while we're at it, we could lower the price of gas to fit our budgetary requirements."

Murph refused to let Charles derail what had started out as a good direction. "How about the error totals and remakes you just mentioned Marti," Murph asked. "What would that entail?"

While it appeared Murph was listening intently to her answer, inside he was partly mad and partly disappointed. Certainly he had seen young men from past teams cost themselves their spots on the team because of some perceived sleight. Why a young man would let misplaced anger push them toward an inevitable and negative outcome never ceased to amaze the old coach. Of course sometimes they had reasons. Coaches were human and made mistakes just like anyone else. Sometimes those mistakes meant a kid got the short end of a stick. Murph believed with all his heart that if there were any reasonable way to solve the problem, coaches, at least his coaches, would find a way.

But this was different. In Charles' case this was a man's life. At Charles' age there would be no other job opportunities. Charles, Murphy assumed, probably had a mortgage, maybe kids in college, car loans, things like that. If Murph couldn't find a way to make this work for all sides, the consequences were much bigger than just not playing a game.

Tuning back in, everyone except Charles was engaged in lively conversation. Almost surprised, the first thought in Murph's head was "excellent." But then he looked at Charles and saw body language that suggested the Cubs might win the World Series before he'd participate. *"Great,"* Murph thought. *"So other than that, how was the play, Mrs. Lincoln?"*

"OK," Murph said. "You've got the idea. I want you to start thinking 'play to win.' Everything, every single thing we do should contribute to that one simple goal. If it doesn't, examine in. Figure out what we can do about it. I imagine we may well find a few inefficiencies here and there. Eliminate them. Keep everything focused on playing to win.

"But, and this is important," Murph added. "Don't stop there. Get your staffs and everyone out there on the front lines to do the same. My guess is that the people who've done the same job for years and years know a lot more about the ins and outs of that job than most of us, and certainly me. Get their input."

Murph looked around the table. Everyone was nodding and making notes.

"Turn the page please."

At the top of the second page was this: ***Be Fair to Employees, Customers and the Company.***

"Back to football," Murph smiled. "We know that in order to have a successful program we have to be fair to our players, our school and our fans. If one became more important than the others, we were in trouble. Or, if we took advantage of one of the three, we were in trouble.

"I think this is much the same thing.

"Our employees have to know that we're not only in the same canoe together, but that we truly care for them. At the same time, we have to make sure that our customers get a fair shake. It seems to me that they'll only be our 'fans' or customers as long as we give them a reason to. That's a choice they'll always have and we would do well to remember that.

"The third spoke in our wheel is the company . . ."

"Here it comes," Charles muttered.

Murph ignored the remark. "If the employees win and the customer wins but the company doesn't, what happens?"

"Depends on the loss, I guess," Dave jumped in. "It could be anything from 'not much' to 'close the doors.'"

"Exactly right," Murph said. "A big part of our job is to ensure that that doesn't happen.

"This has to be good for us as employees, for our

paying customers and for the company who makes it all possible.

"Any questions?"

As Murph looked around the room he saw some positive signs. During a film session it was obvious when the light finally went on for the freshman who suddenly "got it." These people were showing signs that they were buying what Murph was selling.

"Page three, please," Murph said. He paused as the sound of turning paper filled the room. The top of the next page said: ***"Share and Focus."***

"Guesses, anybody?"

No hands shot up immediately. Finally, Oscar spoke up a bit timidly. "Maybe something to do with sharing the football?" his voice trailing off.

Murph chuckled a little. "Good guess, Oscar, but not exactly.

"What I mean is that we need to share our goals and our results with everyone."

"Everyone?" Charles asked incredulously.

"Everyone," Murph smiled. "I want to see charts and posters in each department that not only show our goals, but shows how we're doing at all times in relation to them."

"But sir," Dave said. "I mean I understand that just because we haven't done it before isn't a very good reason now, but some of those numbers have been pretty confidential."

"I understand," Murph said reassuringly. "And Mr. Smith and I have talked about that very subject. Does anyone have any idea why numbers are always confidential?"

"I supposed it's because you don't want your competitor knowing," Billy said.

"That's a good answer, Billy," Murph said. "But why, does anyone know that? Think about it. Who exactly are we talking about? Are we talking about the guy who works on the front line for our competitor? Are we talking about the line manager? The plant manager? The owner? Doesn't it make sense that at a certain level, most folks can make pretty educated guesses on numbers? Shoot," he chuckled, "we used to do the same thing in football with our playbooks. But we all pretty much run the same plays and by halftime there's really not very many surprises.

"At any rate, Mr. Smith doesn't mind sharing information. I think he said something about the numbers might actually make people feel sorry for him.

"He was kidding," Murph smiled. "I think."

"Yeah," Charles snorted. "Real sorry."

Again, Murph ignored the remark and kept going.

"I want all of us working for the same goals and the only way I see that happening is by sharing everything. When we do, we'll be able to get people to focus on the right things. If we focus on the right things, we'll get results."

By now, most of the senior staff was getting the routine and Murph caught more than a couple sneaking a look at the fourth page. Murph made eye contact with Denise and smiled as she almost blushed.

"Turn to page four please."

It read:
Reward Achievements, Respect Efforts.

"When football practice started each fall, we'd have about 100

MURPH'S PLAYBOOK

Although it's all connected with learning how to play to win, this is an important point. In sports, as in business, if the team spends its time focusing on the wrong things, the team has a much smaller chance of succeeding. It's the job of the leader to ensure that the team focuses on the right things.

COACHING SUCCESS

guys competing for 24 spots – sometimes 23 if the kicker and punter turned out to be the same guy. For the most part, that's 100 determined and highly trained and motivated individuals," Murph explained. "Not all of them were going to get what they wanted though. Almost to a man, over all those years, they all wanted the same thing – to start. And see, they were used to it. Most of them had been a player of star caliber in high school or else they wouldn't even entertain the idea of playing college ball. Most had been recruited by several schools. Regrettably, some had even been told by some of those schools that they guaranteed them playing time or a starting job.

"Ultimately, you've got about 80 guys who try their guts out – oops, sorry if I got a bit too graphic there. But they give it their all. Some are just better than others though and those are the ones who end up with one of those coveted 23 or 24 spots.

"The others, though, are still important members of the team. Some are capable backups and will wind up playing almost as many minutes as the starters. Others, well, others you just know are going to come out there every day and sweat and work and bust their tail and, if they're lucky, may get to play a couple of minutes here and there. You've got to respect and appreciate the efforts they put into it. They are all important members of the team. I've had teams with guys who hardly ever got into a game because their talents just weren't good enough. But they still contributed during practice and they still helped make that team a better one at the end of the day.

"Now I realize this isn't school and we don't give high marks just for trying. We pay people for results out here. But seems to me there're a lot of parallels. We've got "starters." We've got reserves. Things change. People move. Spots open. While we need to reward those who consistently achieve and really are a part of us playing to win, we need to respect the efforts of everyone.

"And this part is important people so write this down," Murph said in a bit more serious tone. "If someone in this plant busts their tail, we're going to work very hard to find a spot for them. If in the end, they just do not have the skills or talents we need, we're going to see if we can teach it. If we can't, we're going to help them do something else in life, but we're going to make sure we do so respectfully.

"Don't get the wrong idea about what I'm saying," Murph explained. "We want and need people who can not just play to win, but who can help everyone win. When someone can't help in that process, this won't be the place they'll retire from. But there's no reason we can't respect their efforts during the process.

"And that leads us to page five."

For a moment, no one turned his or her pages. The silence took Murph back a second until he realized that everyone was writing. As he looked around at his newest team, he could tell – by the body language, by the heads nodding, by the looks they gave each other – that he was reaching them.

"OK, maybe before we get into page five, we ought to take a quick break," Murph said. "What do you think?"

"I'm fine." "Me, too." "Thanks, but no," comments rolled around the table.

Murph stifled a smile, but then noticed that Charles was scooting his chair back.

"OK then, we'll forge on," Murph said before Charles could get up. Although Charles' sigh was audible across the length of the table, Murph enjoyed the little victories when he could get them.

Page five said *"Active Accountability."*

"In college, it's different," Murph said. "We don't have the luxury here of saying effort alone is good enough. In school, even if the effort didn't result in increased talent, the only penalty was being a little lower on the depth chart. In grade school, the only penalty was a bad grade.

But here in the working world, sometimes effort isn't enough. We have to have results."

"So you're saying we fire anyone who makes a mistake or doesn't have the talent you think they need to be a *starter*," Charles said, letting sarcasm drip all over the word "starter."

"No, not at all," Murph said patiently. "First mistakes are different and we'll talk about those more a little later. But if someone really tries and fails to perform at acceptable levels, firing isn't even an option. Again, we're not talking about a kid finding out they are sitting on the bench while playing a game. We're talking about real life and real consequences.

"So, our first duty is to find out whey they aren't performing. Is there some outside reason over which they have no control? Did we teach them the proper technique? Did we train them well? What's the reason? In football, we practice on the field four days a week during the season. We play a game one day and we watch film one day and we – well, at least the players – have one day off. If a player isn't playing to the level we need – either in a game or in practice, the coaches break down the reasons why and devise a plan to correct the problem. It could be something as simple as we need to correct a technique. The coaches will spend extra time in practice or maybe after practice to work with that young man.

"That's what I want you to do," Murph continued. "When one of our team doesn't perform to acceptable standards, be active and hold them accountable. Then find out why and work with them to correct the problem."

"What happens if that doesn't correct the problem," Billy asked.

"Option two, ask for help," Murph answered.

"So we're going to spend all this time making everyone all-American football players," Charles snorted. "Yeah, we've got time for that!"

"I imagine when it comes right down to it, Charles,"

Murph said, impressing most everyone with his patience, "that it will take less time and money to work on correcting the problem and improving the employee than either the down time we'll have if we fire them and the decreased productivity and expense of hiring someone new, or the expense of holding onto someone who can't do the job."

Murph swore he saw a few people around the table hiding smiles at that.

"Look, we've been here a long time today and we've covered the five points I wanted to cover," Murph went on. "Let's plan on having this meeting once a week so we can ensure we all stay on the same page.

"I know I'm talking about doing things a little differently than what you've all been used to, and I can't tell you how much I appreciate your patience today and your willingness to work with me. I've got to tell you, I'm pretty excited about our possibilities."

As everyone started getting up to leave, most stopped by and told Murph what a good meeting it was or that they enjoyed listening to him – most everyone, except Charles. Murph was getting used to seeing Charles' backside as it went through a door.

Chapter **4**

All the way home, Charles stewed and steamed. He just could not understand why he was once again getting screwed by the company. After all, he only had another couple of years until he was going to retire. Why bring in "another" new boss? Another one who – Charles was sure – was told to either run Charles off or to make his life so miserable that he'd quit.

Well, he'd show the bastards. If they fired him he'd go out and find a good attorney and he end up owning that damn company. If they thought they could run him off, well, they didn't know much about Charles Jones. He'd found ways to stick it to a lot better bosses than this one. A football coach? What the hell were they thinking anyway?

Charles pulled into the drive just a little too fast, causing the tires to squeal a tiny bit. From inside the 1960's style tri-level, his wife heard the all-too-familiar screech and knew her husband was in another one of his moods. Why couldn't they just leave him alone, she wondered? They were going to kill him with all the stress they loaded on top of him every day. The poor dear had shown up faithfully every day for the past 42 years. Wasn't that enough?

The door slammed as Charles huffed into the living

room. "You won't believe what they did to me today," he started, only pausing long enough to toss his coat on the chair as he headed toward the bar for a strong whiskey and coke.

For the next 90 minutes Charles pored through every detail, every perceived slight, every nuance that he was sure was directed at him personally. As the conversation always went, it didn't take him long before past issues were brought back to life all over again. Some, more than five or 10 years old, still got his blood boiling all over again. Although his wife understood and was clearly on his side, she also knew better to suggest that he let go of some of that anger. She had made that mistake years before and then had to endure the fury directed at her. No, she wasn't about to jump in and suggest to her husband of more than 40 years that he let it go. Better that he direct his rage at them than her. After all, they're the ones who deserve it.

The radio played an easy instrumental from the 1950's as Marti hummed along. The day at the plant was long forgotten as she enjoyed a leisurely drive home. She knew she still had to stop at the grocery. Her husband hated to do the shopping, so she took care of it. The list from the fridge was already tucked into her purse. Most of the staples were on it, as well as a few "extras:" ice cream and some sweets. She knew that her husband didn't really need it, especially since the doctor told him he needed to drop a few pounds at his last physical. But it made him happy. And that in turn made her happy. The first song ended and a favorite from Doris Day followed.

The drive home was fairly uneventful for Dave. He was a little worried . . . no, worried wasn't the right word. He was "aware" that things were about to change quite a bit at work. He wasn't completely sure if that would end up being a good thing or a bad thing. He thought that this Murphy fellow was a straight shooter and an overall good guy. But whether or not that meant things were going to get better was an altogether different thing. "Good guy" didn't necessarily mean competent. Still it wouldn't hurt at all for Dave to make sure he was on Murph's good side. It was a practice that had served him well for most of his career.

By the time he pulled in the driveway, it was almost time to take off again. Larissa was walking toward the mini-van with Sharika in tow. They were on their way to clarinet lessons. Jamal would be at ball practice and would need to be picked up in half an hour. That gave Dave just enough time to hug and kiss his two girls hello and goodbye, change his clothes and start his second full-time – and his most favorite – job: Dad.

Denise, unlike most of her peers, wasn't on the way home. Home was just an apartment where she didn't spend that much time. Tonight would find her at a meeting of her study group. Denise had decided to take advantage of a company-sponsored tuition plan and get her master's degree. Of course when she wasn't busy with class or studies, she was usually taking part in a leadership organization she belonged to. Or once a month there was the young Republican's meeting. There was also infrequent trips to the YWCA where she did lap swimming – although not as often as she liked. There was never enough time for everything, she thought, wondering where the hours went.

Bea was on her way to meet her husband for dinner at a new restaurant in town. She and Chad had to try out the new places, although they certainly had their favorites among the tried and true eating establishments in town.

The parking lot wasn't as full as she expected when she pulled in. Hope that's not a bad sign, she thought as she parked near Chad's SUV. At least he had gotten there first, thus saving her the hassle of waiting in line for a table – she hoped!

Tim Timmons

Making her way through a surprising crowd, she found Chad waiting in a booth. He got up and gave her a quick kiss.

"Hey hon, how was work?" he asked.

"Interesting," she said, setting across the table from him, "The new boss is going to either fail spectacularly or really turn things around. I haven't decided which way I think it'll go yet."

They talked for another minute or two about work. She shared a story or two, as did he. With that out of the way, they spent the next two hours enjoying some new and pleasant Italian dishes and the company of each other's best friend.

Billy walked into the house and immediately smelled supper. He couldn't make it out, but it was good, whatever it was. He walked into the kitchen and gave his wife a quick peck on the cheek and a pat a little lower.

"How was your day, Mr. Polaski?"

"Long," he sighed. "I honestly don't know if they could keep the doors to the place open if it wasn't for me." Settling his large girth into a chair at the table, he looked toward the stove. "What's for supper, Mrs. Polaski?" he asked in the same exact way he had asked every night for the last 20 years.

"I knew, what with a new plant manager and all, that it would be a hard day," she said. "So I made your favorite, liver and onions.

"Honestly," she said, switching gears. "I don't know why that Mr. Smith couldn't have put you in charge to run the place. There isn't anyone there nearly as good as you are."

"I know," Billy nodded. "I don't know anyone, anywhere who could do it as well as me, you know," Billy said. "I hate to sound like I'm tooting my own horn, but it gets frustrating when everyone else makes so many mistakes. There's just no one accountable there. Oh, they say they are, but they screw up and then someone in my department, or more often, me, ends up having to fix it. And the one who screwed it up just walks away scot free."

Billy Polaski's wife shook her head as she turned the sizzling liver. She couldn't understand how all the other people at that plant could be so incompetent.

Joseph Cox was sitting in his study reading that day's editorial from one of the New York newspapers. The walls, a dark wood panel, held some very prestigious marks of achievement from some of America's finest schools. There was no doubt that Joseph was a very educated and learned man. While he sat there reading, his wife was busy in the utility room changing a fuse that had blown. It wasn't the sort of task she could ever ask Joseph to do – maybe if his name were Joe, but Joseph had never shown the interest or aptitude to do anything mechanical or practical. Consequently, his wife handled most of the jobs around the house.

One of Joseph's peers, Oscar, was working – or more factually, trying not to – on a similar project at his house. Oscar's wife had been bugging him for what seemed like an eternity to fix whatever it was that caused the kitchen sink to leak. It was just another project that Oscar could do if he had to, but hated. First off, it was difficult for a guy his size to get under the sink. Second, he would rather grab some chips and a cold one and watch the game – and it didn't even matter which game.

As soon as he walked in the door that night, his wife was all over him.

"You promised," she had almost screamed. "It needs to get done and it needs to get done tonight." Apparently, she had almost knocked over the bucket that held all the water that had leaked under the sink. Well, maybe he could get away with just dumping the water and making some noise. That might get him back to his easy chair a little quicker.

TJ hardly even noticed anything on the drive home. The wheels in his head were spinning at 100 miles per hour. First, there were some real possibilities in that plant. But then there was Charles – Murph wondered if he had ever been called Chuck – and his whole set of issues. The key, Murph thought, was getting everyone to take him and his plans seriously. Did they agree with his five points? Did they think he was nuts? It was hard to tell. On the other hand, if they were a little slow to jump on board with his five points, what would they think of his next step? Sheesh! He almost thought it would be easier to prepare his old Huskies to play Notre Dame – and he *knew* how that one would turn out!

Julie smiled as Murph walked in the door and went straight to his den. He had done the same thing about a thousand other times, but it had been a few years, she thought. In fact, she couldn't remember the last time she had seen him this excited about anything. Other wives might look at that differently, but a coach's wife knew.

It was the fastest week Murph could remember. Names and faces turned into a blur. He found that it was a lot easier to learn names when the first 20 times he saw someone, their name was written in magic marker on a piece of tape on the front of their helmet. Murph spent most of the week learning the layout of the plant. He made sure he was out on the front lines. He asked questions. He answered questions straight and honest. He even took a turn here and there doing jobs. He found that when given half a chance, people were proud to show the coach or the boss – those two titles were

> **MURPH'S PLAYBOOK**
>
> *Coaches don't sit behind desks. They get out on the practice field. They teach. They correct. They take part. Players actually enjoy the times when a coach "plays." It's the same in business.*

becoming intertwined in Murph's mind – what they did and how they did it. All in all, people took pride in what they did.

Although it didn't surprise Murph to see that, it did relieve him greatly. Much of what he had planned depended a great deal on people's basic desire to be the best. When he asked one of the machinists to explain the difference between two different jobs on the bench, Murph was sure to take the time to listen and absorb what the man was telling him. Murph knew he really didn't need to walk away an expert in metal fabrication, but he did have to leave the machinist with the understanding that Murph respected what the man did for a living – and just as important – that Murph appreciated him for it.

As Murph made his way between departments, that personal interaction wasn't lost on any of the senior staff that accompanied him – with the exception of one. Charles figured the new boss could work his way around just fine on his own. So as Murph spent time in Charles' area, he did so on his own. In a way, it turned out better because Murph was able to see a lot of problems that Charles could've kept hidden. For example, the first thing that Murphy noticed was people who wouldn't make eye contact. That was strange, he thought. What do they have to be afraid of? When Murphy tried to talk to a woman who worked at a computer, he got one-word answers to almost all of his questions. When Murphy thanked her for her time and walked off, she seemed almost relieved. The more time he spent there, the more he became convinced that these people were afraid of senior management. And that angered him. No one anywhere at any time should fear someone in a job. Charles was going to be a much bigger challenge than Murphy had previously thought – and Murphy had thought he was going to be a pretty big one.

Tim Timmons

The following Monday, everyone – even Charles – was on time for the next meeting between Murph and senior staff. There was a definitive feeling of energy this time. The apprehension was mostly gone. Although not much had changed with Charles, the rest of the team was beginning to come together nicely.

Even with that, Murph was more worried about this meeting than he was the first one. In retrospect, the first one had been as easy as an intrasquad scrimmage. This felt almost like the season opener. They had a few practices under their belt and now it was time to step up. And with what Murph had in mind, he hoped this didn't turn into a blowout.

"Good afternoon, everyone," Murph smiled, noticing that everyone, including Charles, had their notebooks out. "First of all, I want to say thank you. I know it's been a strain for you to all 'baby-sit' the boss, and I really appreciate it. The time I've been able to spend in your departments has been invaluable to me."

Dave Eads was quick to jump in.

"Honestly, Mr. Murphy, it was a good thing for everyone," Dave was saying was a lot of enthusiasm. "My folks haven't stopped talking about it. If you don't do anything else, the boost you gave the morale in the plant was worth it."

Murph knew that a lot of what Eads said had to be taken with a grain of salt. He thought the big man's intentions were good, but he also recognized someone who was trying to butter up the coach. It hadn't worked for any players over a whole lot of years and Murph didn't figure it would change much now. Even so, Murph had to admit that with Charles' constant sarcasm and backbiting, a little sucking up did create a bit of a balance.

"Thanks, Dave," Murph smiled. "But I think the morale will take care of itself when the results get better . . . which is exactly what I want to talk about today." Immediately, notebooks were opened and pens picked up.

COACHING SUCCESS

The team was indeed ready. In fact, the quickness and attentiveness caught the old coach a little off guard.

"OK then, I want to share some observations and then set up where we go from here," Murph continued. "The more I walked around the plant and the more time I spent with all of our folks the more optimistic I became. It looks to me like we have a great many people here who want to do a first-rate job. I saw pride. I saw excitement. But, I saw frustration with outdated equipment. I saw confusion. And I saw some apathy."

The staff looked at Murphy. Although they knew there were problems, it was still disappointing to hear that the new boss concurred. In fact, the only one at the table who was finally nodding in agreement was Charles. From his perspective, maybe now this football coach would realize that he was in way over his head. Of course the perspective at the head of the table was anything but that.

"I don't know if it's an omen or just convenient, but today's the first day of the month," Murph said. "It seems a perfect day to start our new plan." With this, Murph leaned forward. It almost seemed as if he was back in the huddle calling the next play, the one that would strike the defense straight in the heart.

"Remember from our last meeting that we are here to play to win. We want to be fair to our employees, our customers and our company. We want to stay focused, reward achievements, respect efforts and hold people accountable. We are going to do that by teaching and training. By making sure we do the basics of each job well so that we can be in a position to be successful. There's more, but you all get the idea."

Heads were nodding.

"So now, especially with today being the first day of a new month and a new financial accounting period, it's time to take our first step."

Murph looked around. Walt Smith had been right

about many things, not the least being that the boss didn't have to prove he/she was the boss. Here Murph was, a life-long football guy. And yet after only a week, these people, people who were infinitely better in this particular industry than Murph was now and likely ever would be, and they were looking to him for direction and leadership. Like Smith said, the only one in the room with doubts was Murph himself – OK, and maybe Charles, too.

What Murph was going to say next though was the part that had him the most nervous. It certainly wasn't something that was a common everyday business practice. In fact, outside of sports, Murph hadn't really heard of this idea. If there was the slightest crack or flaw in the plan, Murph knew that Charles would run all over it, kind of like a linebacker who suddenly finds no one between him and the quarterback. But, Murph didn't think there was a flaw in this plan. Was it different? Sure. Different didn't necessarily mean bad though.

"We have a brand new year," Murph started out. "It's a new year and a new and fresh start. My intent, and what I want our intent to be, is to "win" at least 10 months."

"What exactly do you mean by win?" Charles asked, surprising Murphy with what sounded like a reasonable question asked in a non-sarcastic tone.

"Good question, Charles," Murph said. "A win or a loss will simply be measured in terms of the bottom line. If we hit our budget, it's a win and goes in the books that way. If we fall short, it's a loss."

"How many times have we "won" in the last year?" Bea asked, afraid she pretty much knew the answer already.

"We have a record of 3-9 the past 12 months," Murph answered honestly. But before anyone could say anything else, he quickly added, "But that does not mean that these next 12 months can't be successful. We are going to help our people find ways to succeed. We, you and me, are going to spend all our time looking for better answers. Did anybody see that movie Apollo 13 with Tom Cruise?"

"Tom Hanks," Bea smiled.

"Sorry," Murph smiled. "My wife knows all that stuff. She just drags me along once in a while. But I remember that those guys in the movie said that failure wasn't an option, and I like that idea for us. Maybe it's not life or death, but it is our job. And I haven't met anyone yet in this plant who's told me they want to fail."

Murph paused and took stock of the staff. At least they weren't running for the doors screaming about the madman who's taken over the plant.

"Look folks, I know we can do . . ."

The interruption wasn't, couldn't have been unexpected. The tone though, once again, was a pleasant surprise.

"What happens if we fail?" Charles asked.

"Or, what happens if we 'win' the majority of the months and still fall short of the year because we missed the biggest months," Bea tossed in.

"Two excellent questions," Murph conceded. "Let me take them in reverse order. First off, I intend to pay everyone in the plant a bonus if we are successful."

That dropped a few jaws.

"The bonus will be contingent upon winning. The size of the bonus will depend on the overall bottom line. However, we will share that information with the plant each month so there's no question as to where we all stand and what we have to do from that point forward. I understand that sharing information like that has not been done in the past," Murph explained before Charles or anyone else could jump in. "However, Walt Smith and I agreed that if we're going to ask folks to do things differently, it starts at the top. Walt has agreed to share with you and with the folks who work here. I think that's a pretty big decision from him."

Murph paused. That was the easy part.

Murphy looked around. He wanted to be very careful at this point. On one hand, he had to get this particular group excited and open to the possibilities. If he couldn't convince these guys, this wasn't going to go very far. On the other hand, if he tried shoving a hokey locker room speech down their throats, he knew that wouldn't work either. As always for Thomas J. Murphy, shooting straight was the best policy. He also knew that they might as well get used to tackling the tough issues head on now. Why wait?

"If we fail?" he repeated, looking at Charles who had first asked the question. "I hate answering a question with a question, but what do you guys think we should do?"

"We should fix the procedures that caused us to fail," Oscar said.

"We should hold people accountable," Dave added.

"We should get rid of the deadwood that caused us to fail," Billy said.

"No, and yes," Bea said. "We should figure out why we failed and take the appropriate action to address those reasons."

"Thanks, Bea," Murph said. "That's exactly what we should do. But I want you to know that I don't think we'll fail. I think we've got the right people and the right circumstances. I think we have a great chance to go 12-0."

Chapter 5

Predictably, the first two months were miserable.

If something could go wrong, it did. Machines broke down. Entire shipments went to the wrong place. Bills were figured incorrectly. Wrong decisions were made. That one in particular didn't bother Murphy. But what did was no one could seem to remember who had made the decision initially or how to find out. What Murph saw was that doing a good job wasn't even a consideration. What was killing them were the people who were just trying to preserve their spot in the plant. Their main purpose, it seemed to Murphy, was justifying their existence. Nothing in the world could've made things more difficult to understand for the former coach. In the life he had just left, each position, whether it was a player or a coach, had a reason for being. No one ever felt like they had to justify their actual job. Certainly players worked on whether or not they moved up or down on the depth chart. But they didn't have to worry that the position

> **MURPH'S PLAYBOOK**
>
> *In sports, each position has a purpose. Each coach has a purpose. That much is clear. Always. Is the same true in business? Many times, it's not.*

itself needed to be protected. After all, it was tough to play football without a quarterback or a center or a linebacker. What had gone on in this building in the past that made these people feel this way, he wondered?

And more importantly, what could he do about it? He didn't have the answer, but he was absolutely certain that the answer was tied to the disastrous results for the first two months.

Part of him wanted to pick up the phone and call Walt Smith. He knew he wouldn't though because it wasn't Smith's job to figure it out. That's why he hired Murphy. Plus, Murphy knew that Smith hadn't spent that much time around the plant. Anything Smith thought would be a guess at best.

Besides, after the results of the first two months, Murphy wasn't real sure he wanted to be on the other end of the phone from Walt Smith. Starting out 0-2 wasn't exactly the plan Murphy had in mind when he was getting ready to accept this job. In fact, 0-2 was very unfamiliar ground to him.

In all the years Murph coached, starting 0-2 was something he had never once experienced. In fact, there were only three seasons in which he didn't win the opening game, a fact that the local sportswriters always paid attention to at least once a year. To say that Murph was miserable would be like saying the Titanic had an incident with a piece of ice. If there was anything that coaching had not prepared him for it was failure. Sure, he had lost games here and there. But he never once had a losing season. It was another one of those facts that sportswriters seemed to hit at least once a year.

Truth to tell though, it *was* pretty unusual for a coach to always win. The worst season Murph ever endured was 6-4. It was probably the one season he identified the most with right now. That team had started the season 2-0, lost three in a row, won another and lost another. With three conference games left the Huskies stood 3-4 and things looked bleak for the home team. In fact, Murph had spent a lot of time thinking about that team lately.

Julie was getting worried about her husband. For the first time, she was actually starting to wonder if he had bitten off more than he could chew. He would get up early and head for the plant. When he returned home half a full day later, he was more tired than she had ever seen him. He would come in and plop down on the coach, slide off his shoes first and then the tie. He always made a crack about "that damn tie." Then he would tell her story after story about why things didn't work that day.

The reasons never seemed to be the same. One day it was a piece of machinery that broke. The next day it was someone forgot something, or the only person with the right information was on vacation that week, or someone thought they were supposed to zig when they should've zagged. All in all, Julie was a little more concerned with each passing day.

"Wait, I think I know the problem," Murph said from the couch with his eyes closed and not a hint of enthusiasm behind the proclamation.

"What is it?"

"You talked me into taking this job," he said deadpan. Then he opened his eyes and smiled so she would know for sure that he was kidding. That he even had to make sure wasn't a great sign.

"You know that you don't have to do this," she said. "You told Walt Smith that you would give it a try. You didn't make any promises and you didn't sign any contracts. I think he's the kind of man who would understand if you told him that this just wasn't working out."

"But dang it, Jules," Murph said. "I've never quit anything in my life."

Murphy wasn't mad at her, she knew. And he certainly didn't sound mad. He was frustrated. If she knew anything at all about her husband after all this time it was that he absolutely hated to lose. He hated it with a passion. Julie believed with all her heart that it was the one feature that kept him head and shoulders above the rest of the coaches in the conference. On those occasions when the Huskies dropped a game, it wasn't at all unusual for Julie to not see or hear from her husband for a day or even two. She never worried. If she needed to reach him, all she had to do was call his office line. If he didn't answer that phone, she called the film room phone. He was always at one or the other, although it was more likely he was breaking down game film. She always felt a little sorry for the assistants during this time. It didn't bother Murph in the least to go all night and well into the next day. He would run the film over and over until he found every tiny reason why the team lost. Then he and his staff would devise a plan for how to overcome whatever the reason so that they would be successful the next . . .

Julie suppressed her smile.

"Have you broke down the film yet?" she asked.

"Huh," Murph murmured, sounding as if he was about ready to doze off. "What film, what are you talking about?"

"Seems to me that when you lost a football game you would break down the film until you knew every single reason why you lost. Then you just fixed those reasons. Have you done that yet?"

Murph sat upright. He really hadn't thought about it in those terms. He was so busy solving this problem or putting out that fire that stepping back and analyzing it all afterward in the darkness of a film room just fell through the cracks. It was important, Murph knew, to get away from the screaming fans and the emotions on the field. It was important to get away from the players who had their own wants and needs. It was important to get the key decision makers away from everything so they could analyze exactly what had happened and why. Then all they had to do was take the information to its logical conclusion and put together a plan for the next week.

Murph actually sprang up from the couch, bounced across the room and took his wife's face between his hands. "I always said that you were the brainy one in the family, Mrs. Murphy," he smiled. "I love you!" And with that, he grabbed the Jeep keys and headed out the door. Julie looked at the clock that was nearing 10 p.m. and sighed. It was going to be another lonely night at the Murphy household.

The next morning all the senior staff had a memo on their desk. It just said that there would be a meeting at 8:15 in the conference room by Murphy's office.

"Maybe he's finally come to his senses and is quitting," Charles said to Billy. "That or else Smith has come to his senses and is firing the s.o.b."

"You're just hoping to snag that job, Charles," Billy said. "You ought to know that that won't happen." Although Billy didn't say he thought the job should belong to him, he didn't have to. Both Charles and Billy knew what Billy thought.

"All I know is the numbers have gotten worse since the great TJ Murphy has come along to 'coach' us," Charles spat out. "I said it was a mistake to bring in a person with no background or product knowledge then and I'll say it again now."

"Yeah, but you won't say it too loud," Billy said. "Right or wrong, I don't think Murphy would hesitate to toss your can out the door."

"Says you," Charles snorted. "First off, they couldn't get anything out of that department without me. Second, I'd slap an age discrimination suit on them so fast it would make their heads spin. By the end of the day, I'd own the company."

Murphy came walking around the corner.

"Good morning Charles, Billy," Murphy said without breaking his brisk stride. "See you guys at the meeting."

Billy almost laughed out loud wondering what, if

anything the boss had heard. Charles just did what he always did – seethed.

Even though Murphy was still fairly new and they were all learning how each other worked, it was a bit unusual to have this sort of impromptu meeting. Someone had thoughtfully filled the large silver coffeemaker and the aroma of fresh coffee filled the conference room. "Someone" had to be Effie, Murphy thought. If there had ever been a more efficient secretary, he couldn't imagine who it might be. He only wished he had Effie around to handle the detail stuff when he was coaching.

Murph was one of the first there and he had his U-of-I coffee cup in hand and was walking around the room talking individually with each member of the senior staff. It was just another one of the traits that put him a notch above the next guy down the totem pole. People truly liked Murph because he took the time to talk to each person, and more importantly, he listened when they talked. After less than 90 days, Murph could list all the spouses of senior staff, children and even most grandchildren. It wasn't something that T.J. Murphy really thought about, but anyone who ever studied human psychology could have told him, when people like someone, they want to do well for them, or at the very least, not disappoint them.

Murph glanced at his watch and checked it against the clock on the wall. They both read 8:20. The meeting was already five minutes late and yet there was no sign of Charles. Just as Murph decided to get started, in he walked. Instead of getting to his seat though, Charles made a show out of going over to get a cup of coffee, thus

> **MURPH'S PLAYBOOK**
> *Being a coach or a boss isn't a popularity contest. However, people work hard for someone they like, and or respect.*

delaying things even more – if only by a little bit.

While they were all waiting, Bea looked closely at Murphy. Something was amiss, she thought, but couldn't place it. She looked closer without trying to be conspicuous. Then she saw it. There were bags under his eyes. Once she noticed it, he clearly looked like he wasn't getting enough sleep. "Poor guy," she thought. "He's really having a tough time with this job."

"Thanks for meeting on such short notice," Murph started after Charles had finally got to his seat. "We're struggling, which of course doesn't tell you anything you don't already know. But why? Why are we struggling? Anyone have the exact answer?"

With that Murph walked over to the board on the wall and wrote, "Why are we struggling?" in big blue letters across the top. He turned and looked around the room.

Everyone looked at their notebooks as if the answer might be there waiting for them. The only one who didn't look down was Charles. He said something that caused those around him to do a double take. Murph was too far away to hear, but he saw the reaction and knew Charles had done something — again. It was getting old.

"Charles, an idea?" Murph asked.

"No, Coach," Charles replied. He had gotten into the habit of calling Murphy "Coach" at every turn. In fact, quite a few people around the plant had as well. Although when Charles said it, it didn't sound quite the same.

"Bea, how about you," Murphy asked.

"Well, to be honest with you, I don't really have one answer," she said. "I mean I can point my finger at this here and that there, but I don't know if it's that simple. Really, it's hard to get your arms around."

"Good point," Murph said. "Anyone else?"

Billy threw out a few things; mostly pointing out how his department was doing better than everyone else and if they would only follow his example then there wouldn't be a problem. Denise and Dave added their two cents. Joseph shared his opinion, although by the time he was done no one was really sure what he had said.

Murphy pointed at the board. "Would it be fair to say that we don't have a definitive answer then?" he asked. Heads nodded. "OK, that's the same conclusion I came to last night after I came back."

Bea looked again at the bags under his eyes. *"My goodness,"* she thought. *"He worked all night!"*

"I want you all to go back to your calendars and see if you can clear out two days within the next 10 days," Murph explained. "Call Effie and give her all the dates where you have two days back to back free. Could you do that within the next hour?"

Everyone nodded.

"Great. What I want to do is what you in business would call an off-site retreat. In coaching, we just called it film," the old coach explained. "The idea will be to get us all out of here for a couple of days. We'll be able, I think, to answer that question an awful lot better when there're no phones ringing, no faxes or e-mails, no employees and no customers. We all need some uninterrupted time so that we can really focus on the issue at hand.

"Any questions?"

Charles raised his hand.

"So Coach, you're asking us to leave our homes for two days as well? Where on earth are we going? I've got grass to cut and a doctor's appointment and lots of things going on, you can't just expect us to take our own time and . . ."

Murph didn't even slow down. "OK, Charles has a good point. Is there anyone here who can't rearrange things on a personal level sometime in the next 10 days or so?"

Charles felt lonely with his being the only hand

raised. Slowly, he lowered it and said, "Well, I guess I'll try to find a way to make do."

"That would be great," Murphy answered. "Now, if you guys can give those dates to Effie, we'll get this show started."

"But you didn't answer Charles' question," Denise asked. "Where are we going?"

"To watch some film, Denise," Murph said. "To watch some film."

Chapter 6

Max was surprised to hear his old friend when he answered the phone.

"So how's the world of high finance?" Max said.

"It's a hell of a lot different than football, I can tell you that," Murph said, also surprised at how good it was to hear Max's voice. "I'm starting to wonder if your new coach might need another assistant or two?"

"Oh c'mon, Coach, it can't be that bad?"

"I don't know" Murph sighed. "Remember that year we finished 6-4?"

"Sure."

"Well, it was a lot more fun than this has been so far."

Max nearly burst out laughing, even if he didn't mean to. "Doggone Coach, I don't believe anybody on campus had any fun during that season. If I remember right, you even had the librarians walking on egg shells!"

"Very funny," Murph said and then added with a laugh, "It was pretty bad though, wasn't it? Listen, I'm calling to ask a favor."

"Name it, Coach. You know I'll do anything I can for you."

"Is the film room open in the next few weeks?"

"Well, sure," Max said, wondering what Murph could want with old film. "We haven't got your replacement quite hired yet and no one's really doing much in there right now. It might be a bit dusty though."

"Great," Murph said. "Do you think I could bring my management team over to the school?"

"Well, sure, Coach, but why?"

"Hold on. You didn't let me finish. I don't want to just bring them over. I want to throw them in dorm rooms for one night and I want to feed them lunch and dinner the first day and breakfast and lunch the next."

"From our cafeteria?"

"Yup."

"What's the matter, you don't like these folks?"

"Aw c'mon," Murph laughed. "The food's not that bad."

"Sure it is," the athletic director said. "You just have a crappy memory."

Effie Perez and the assistants for all the department heads had their hands full trying to coordinate all the schedules. Each department head had a list of cancellations and calls that needed to be made on short notice. One thing was for certain. Whatever Effie's boss was up to clearly had everyone buzzing. However, when it came to getting something organized, there wasn't any doubt that Effie was the right person for the job. She just wished she knew a little more about what was going to happen.

Murphy had given her an itinerary to type. It didn't provide that many answers.

8 a.m.	Report to Room 321 on campus at University of Indiana to receive room assignments. Escort to room and unpack
9 a.m.	Meet back in Room 321
11 a.m.	Lunch
1 p.m.	Meet back in Room 321
6 p.m.	Supper
8 a.m.	Meet back in Room 321
11 a.m.	Lunch
1 p.m.	Meet back in Room 321

Tim Timmons

The evening before he was to lead his team to U of I, Julie Murphy liked the extra bounce she detected in her husband's step. Although she knew he still had a challenge ahead of him, she was pleased to see a lot of the old Murph emerging from the funk of the last couple of months.

"You know, Jules, I think I've got an awful lot of this figured out," Murph said. He was sitting in his recliner; one of two matching chairs the Murphys had bought years before.

"What's that, dear?" she asked – as if she didn't know what he was talking about.

"I've been going over these figures and I think if we just . . . "

Murphy was on a roll and his wife was nodding her head. It wasn't that she didn't want to listen. On the contrary, she loved hearing him like this. The old excitement was there. There was a fire in his belly. And that's what truly made him the happiest. And she loved seeing him happy.

". . . and I think that gets us a big step in the right direction," Murph finished.

"That sounds just fine to me," Julie Murphy said from her recliner.

Murph felt awfully odd walking from the parking lot to the athletic building. First off, he didn't park in his old spot. He had been parking in the same spot ever since he came to Noblesville. Not today though. Although that job didn't belong to anyone else just yet, Murphy knew it wasn't *his* anymore. Then as he walked across campus, everything just felt different. About the only thing that was the same was the dew on the ground. Although the meeting didn't start until 8, Murph was getting in around 6. He knew Max was already there, just like always. The two former colleagues would share a cup of coffee and get the day started. Only this day was going to be a great deal different than any of the ones they had shared before.

COACHING SUCCESS

Another thing that felt different was the steps to the third floor. He didn't remember there being this many steps, or them being so steep!

"G'morning Coach," Max cheerfully called out when Murph walked in.

"G'morning," Murph said as he dropped his gym bag and briefcase by the door and headed for the coffee pot.

"So, pardon me for being a little confused here, Coach," Max said. "I thought you had left the coaching job behind for the big bright world of business."

"Huh?" Murph said, missing the playful jab.

"You didn't tell me you were not only coming back but bringing a whole new staff with you," Max said. "Geez though, Coach, I wish they had a little more experience."

"Very funny," Murph said.

"And women coaching football . . ." Max went on without skipping a beat. "I guess we'll have to find some sort of locker room arrangement for them . . ."

As Max kept the needling going, Murph found another difference between football and business – camaraderie. He hadn't realized how much he missed it until now. Sure, Max was having some fun at Murphy's expense, but it was all in fun.

When it came right down to it, there wasn't any question that he and Max and all the former assistants were all on the same team. He also realized that that spirit, that willingness to support each other, to work hard for each other, to celebrate in the successes together and to lean on each other during the failures – all those things were pretty common in every successful team Murphy had been

> **MURPH'S PLAYBOOK**
>
> *Sports has a very serious side to it. Yet, it's still fun. Why isn't business and what can you do to make it that way?*

around. It was one of the big missing ingredients with his new team. Try as he might, he had not been able to get them all pulling for the same thing. Why? That's one of the things he was there to find out.

"Very funny," Murph said when his old friend was done. "You know you missed your calling in life, you should've been a comedian. I would say you could've been the next Red Skeleton, but I think you were probably around before Red got started."

"That's not true," Max countered so fast he almost spilled his coffee, which got another laugh out of the two.

"So, what's the game plan today, Coach?"

"Well, I've got to find a way to get us all on the same play," Murph answered. "So far, that's the big thing holding us back. I mean we get one or two things right and then we bumble something else. It's always two steps forward and one step back. Sometimes, it's one forward and two back, you know. The thing is, it's not that tough. I mean the basic premise is we make things, we sell them, we ship them and we provide support. But we too often don't make them right, we don't get them sold, we don't get the shipments to the customer on time and we make the support hard to get. Doesn't seem like it should be that hard to fix, huh?"

Max laughed out loud. "What it really sounds like, Coach, is that getting an 18-year-old 200-pound kid to block some 22-year-old 300-pounder might be a heck of a lot easier."

"You have no idea, Max, no idea."

At 7:40 that morning, Murphy's senior staff started to arrive. Marti Beech was the first to pull up. She looked at the printed map and instructions that Effie Perez gave each of them. Marti pulled her overnight bag from the backseat of the car and started to walk toward the building. She paused when she saw Denise and Joseph pull in the parking lot.

COACHING SUCCESS

"A pleasant good morning," Marti said as Denise and Joseph got their bags out of the respective cars as well.

"We'll see if it's a pleasant morning or not," Denise said warily. "I'm not at all sure about any of this."

"Oh, I've been through this sort of thing before," Joseph said in his usual monotone. "When I was in my last job we used to do all sorts of off-site retreats."

"What did you do at them," Marti asked.

"Nothing good," Joseph mumbled.

The three began walking together.

Surprisingly, Charles was the next to arrive. He actually squealed his tires coming into the lot. Marti, Joseph and even Denise walked a little faster. If Charles was going to start out this way, they didn't want to be around.

One by one, all the participants arrived. When they walked toward Room 321 they found Effie waiting outside the door for them with a map and a key. The map showed them directions to their dorm rooms. They were instructed to get their stuff unpacked and be back ready to go at 9.

When they returned, Room 321's door was closed. There was no Effie waiting this time. Oscar Torres was the first one back, even though he was breathing pretty hard from the walk. Not knowing whether or not he should go in, he stood there for a moment. Then came Dave and Denise walking together. Joseph wasn't far behind. Further back was Billy, Marti and, surprisingly, Charles. Bea was going to be the last one this time, which relieved Oscar a little. He, like everyone, was pretty tired of the little games Charles was playing.

"Hey Oscar," Marti said.

"Marti."

"Why in the world are we all standing out here," Charles said.

"I don't know," Dave answered. "Do you think we're supposed to go on in?"

"Well it beats standing here," Denise said as she reached for the door.

The light from the hall cast an elliptical triangle inside the darkened room. The lack of light caught Denise and the rest by surprise and everyone stopped for just a second.

"Well, come on in," Murph said from the darkness.

For just a second, everyone still hesitated, unsure.

The laughter they heard was from Bea, who obviously wasn't last. "Come on in you guys," she said. "I can't see this film with the door open."

One by one they all filed in and started to look around as their eyes adjusted to the room.

One wall was filled with what looked like gray metal racks, the kind you might find in a garage or a basement. Each one was packed with what looked like books. There were chairs here and there throughout the room, most were old but looked, well, comfortable. The room had a smell that was something between a disinfectant and something stale. Most of the guys in the group recognized it as a locker room smell. The women thought of something less pleasant.

"Find a chair," Murph said from near what was a large screen of some sort at the front of the room. He was outlined as a silhouette against what was obviously some sort of a telecast or film from a football game. Although it was in color, it still looked old somehow. "Bea and I were just taking a look back at one of my old teams."

"Reliving the glory days, coach?" Charles tossed out as he settled into one of the bigger and fluffier chairs.

"Not quite," Murph laughed. "This team actually had a losing record of 3-4."

"But I thought that I read that you never had a losing team," Dave said.

"We didn't," Murph answered. "But this was the eighth game in a 10 game season and before it was played we were 3-4. Matter of fact, we were behind 7-0 at halftime of this one."

"What happened?" Marti asked, evoking a loud sigh from Charles' side of the room.

"We came back and won this game 8-7," Murph said. "We then slipped past Tech and finished with a close victory in the annual Sledgehammer game.

"It was a record of 6-4, and you know what?" Murph asked the group, but didn't wait for an answer. "That was probably the best coaching job any of us ever did."

"But I thought you had a couple of undefeated teams?" Dave asked.

"We did," Murph said. "But those teams had tremendous talent. Heck, the only way we were going to lose a game that one year was if I screwed it up myself.

"But this team that was 6-4, that was a team that very easily could've lost all 10 games. And it's for sure that when they were 3-4 that they shouldn't have won the last three. But they all knew that was the only way we could have a winning record, and that was a big deal to those seniors and those players. They didn't want to leave this school as the only group to ever post a losing record. Heck, they didn't even want to finish .500. They all knew that three weeks and three victories was the only way they could go out of here on their terms. And they worked harder than any team, showed more heart and more determination than any group I've ever been associated with."

With that, Murph turned back to the screen and pointed a remote at the screen. A player wearing No. 24 was running with the ball through the line. He broke one, then two and then a third tackle before several guys in different jerseys finally pulled him down.

"That was a kid who just wouldn't quit," Murph pointed out. "He wasn't the fastest tailback we ever had and he wasn't the strongest. But he never fumbled and he made the other guy bring his best game."

"What's he do now, pro ball?" Charles asked, knowing

that not many kids from U of I went on to the pros.

"He's a doctor now, Charles," Murph said still looking at the screen. "He wasn't the smartest kid in his class either, but he was the hardest worker."

The room was quiet for a minute. Three-fourths of the room was just wishing that Charles would let this feud go while the other two had very different takes on what was happening. Charles could feel himself getting madder by the minute. Murphy just felt a sadness that he was determined not to let anyone else see.

With that, Murph pointed the remote back at the screen and the picture disappeared while lights came on overhead. Everyone did what people always do when the lights come on, straighten up a little, squint and look around.

Murph walked to the front of the room and pulled over a large dry erase board that was on wheels. Grabbing a blue marker, Murph wrote at the top of the board in large letters: What's holding us back from being successful? He then turned and looked everyone over.

"Here's the drill," Murph started. "I know that you all did a lot of juggling to get here and spend this time, and I want you to know how much I appreciate it. Back when I was a coach, we used to come in here after games and look at what we did wrong and what we did right. We broke down all the mistakes and formulated plans to address those issues so that we could move forward. We also broke down what we did right and figured out how we could continue to do so. The practices we did during the week, for the most part, came from the time we spent here after each game.

"So, just what the hell does that have to do with us? Simple. We're going to do the same thing. We're going to break down all the things that are holding us back and we're going to figure out how we create ways around those things. We're going to figure out what we do well and make sure we continue doing that.

COACHING SUCCESS

"This will happen over two days during four different sessions," Murph continued, holding everyone's attention. "At the end of the fourth session, we're going to have a very detailed plan that we're taking back to the plant for immediate implementation."

"Haven't we already been doing that?" Charles asked.

"To some degree, yes," Murph answered. "But we are constantly reacting to some new fire that needs to be put out. We're abandoning our plans because some new problem crops up. We're not being proactive; we're being reactive. In football terms, that means we don't have our own game plan. That means we're just chasing around after the other guy."

"I'm sick and tired of this crap about football!" Charles literally screamed. "All we do is talk about football this and football that. I'm going to tell you 'Coach' that this isn't football. This is real life and real business and you have no idea what you're doing. I can't, I won't stay here and take part in any more of these stupid games. This is getting us nowhere and I won't waste my time. I'm going back to my job and do some real work while you sit over here and try to pretend you know what the hell you're doing."

As Charles slammed the door behind him on the way out, everyone just sat there in disbelief and shock.

Everyone except Effie, that is. She calmly walked over to the phone on the wall, picked it up, punched a few numbers and matter of factly said, "Well, the good news is we'll save a few extra bucks on the meals."

In spite of everything, the room broke up.

However, Murph quickly restored order and looked at each of the remaining senior staff. "It's my job to deal with this and I will, but before we go anywhere else with all this, you need to decide if Charles has a point. If you think all this is a load of crap and, more importantly, if you think I'm leading this company astray, now's the time to say so. I promise that there will be no repercussions for you in this. But it seems silly to go through all this if you don't believe in it."

The next few moments seemed like the longest moments of Murph's career. It reminded him of that last game of the season for the team Murphy had just been talking about a few minutes before. That game had been decided by a two-point conversion after time expired. Murph vividly remembered standing on the sideline and sending in the play – an end-around for old No. 24 – and then watching helplessly as everything unfolded in front of him. Murphy had seen the defensive end cheating toward the middle more and more as the day went on and he was fairly certain the play would work. But from the moment the ball was snapped until No. 24 crossed the goal line with the winning score, time seemed to slow down. That's how he felt right now – helpless, alone, nervous, unsure how the play would turn out.

"Coach, I can't say I *entirely* disagree with Chuck," Denise started as Murph's heart caught in his throat. "But while I do have some trouble relating to all this football stuff, I've got to say that most of what you've been saying makes sense. I sure wouldn't want to give up now after all this."

"Me neither," Dave said. The rest chimed in, too.

"I didn't really have any doubts before," Bea said. "But I'll tell you this. I'll bust my tail now just to prove that blowhard wrong."

Murph realized that he had been holding his breath. He let it out and recovered enough to say something about not wanting to talk more about Charles at this point and that he would handle it later. As usual, the efficient Effie was right there to hand out notepads and pencils.

"Right," Murph said. "I want to talk specifics about what's holding us back. But first, there're a couple of ground rules that we all need to remember for the next two days. First, none of this is personal. If you see some-

COACHING SUCCESS

thing I'm doing that's holding us back, throw it out. I won't be mad. I won't be hurt. I want to know. Second, total honesty. I respect Charles for speaking his mind. If we're going to make this work, you all need to be brutally honest as we go through this. Everyone OK with that?"

There were nods all around.

"Fine, let's get to work."

For the next two hours, the group filled up the large dry erase board and Effie produced an easel with a flip chart. She wrote as fast as she could and Murph helped tape the torn off sheets on the walls. The group talked about how the organization was slow to react. They pointed out that the training programs weren't good enough. Rewards didn't match responsibilities. Reviews and appraisals were a joke. Communication between departments wasn't good enough. Too much time was spent every day on e-mails. Managers didn't hold people accountable because they thought it would cause a problem with morale if they did.

> **MURPH'S PLAYBOOK**
>
> *Honesty is another key trait of successful sports teams. Coaches and players know when someone either isn't giving their all, or are getting beat by a superior opponent. It isn't about hurt feelings or political correctness, nor should it be.*

The list went on and on. The give and take was very honest and for the first time in a couple of months Murph actually felt like progress was being made. Effie's announcement that lunch was in 15 minutes actually came as a surprise. The group was starting to wind down and the break was coming at a perfect time.

"Wow," Murph started. "Congratulations to each of you. This," he said with a wave of his hand at the papers all over the room, "is a great diagnosis of where things are going wrong. Tomorrow, we'll figure out how we do something about it."

"Tomorrow?" Bea asked. "What are we doing this afternoon?"

"Well first Bea, we're going to eat," Murph answered.

"What's for lunch anyway," Billy asked.

"We're all heading over to the cafeteria," Murph said.

"What's the matter, you don't like us," Bea quipped.

"Everybody's a comedian," Murphy groaned.

Murph had already decided that he wouldn't sit with his team at lunch. He figured they either already had their fill of him by then, or they would soon reach that point. At any rate, he had some business to take care of.

"Effie, I need a favor. Have we ever suspended anyone before?"

"Sure," she answered. "HR puts the terms of the suspension in writing and they'll take Chuckie a letter saying such and he'll be out of there before he can do any real damage."

"Uh," Murph stuttered for a second as Effie once again caught him off guard. "I mean how did you . . . well, I guess it's kind of obvious, huh?"

"You bet," she said. "All I need is the go ahead and it'll be a done deal."

"How can it be?" Murph asked. "I haven't even decided anything yet."

"I've already drafted the letter on my laptop," Effie said, surprising Murph once again. "You need to look at it. If it's wrong or it's not what you want, I'll fix it and then I'll call HR, e-mail it to them and they'll get Charles the letter this afternoon. I figured you wouldn't want him running loose in the plant for two days while everyone else is gone. The damage that man would do . . ."

"Effie, how in the world did I get lucky enough to get you for a secretary?"

"I don't know, Coach, just remember that flattery and time off works wonders with me."

Back in the cafeteria, the group was buzzing.

"I can't believe how fast the time flew by this morning," Marti said.

"I can't believe how many problems we identified," said Joseph.

"I can't believe Charles," Oscar said. "Do you think he still works here?"

"He wouldn't if it was me," Bea said.

"But they can't fire him," Billy said. "He's in the protected status as far as age."

"Age protects a lot of things," Denise said. "But I don't think it protects career suicide."

Murph walked up to the table and looked at his watch. "You guys ready for Round Two?" he asked.

Chapter 7

When they walked back into the film room, it looked like they hadn't even been there yet. All the taped up sheets were gone and a clean dry erase board had the following: What do we do right? What do we do better than anyone else?

"OK, this afternoon we're looking for the opposite of this morning," Murph started. "It's easy to find the faults, but if we go back and concentrate on just fixing those, the things that we do well will get lost in the shuffle and we'll actually end up worse. If a football team needs to work on the running game, they don't stop practicing the pass. So, what do we do really, really well?"

The group took this question in mid-stride. Answers flew back and forth fast enough that Effie was having some difficulty in keeping up. The group thought there was a strong desire to succeed. The equipment in the plant was in good shape and there were no need for any major capital expenditures on the horizon. The core group of the mid-level managers had potential. Although they needed more customers, the ones they had tended to be very loyal. The owner was someone who cared about the employees and the community.

Once again, time flew past and Effie's announcement that supper was in half an hour caused heads to turn to wristwatches in surprise. As the group started winding down, Murph caught himself looking around the room. He had spent many, many hours in here with a group of men who gave 100 percent of themselves to a cause they all fiercely believed in. Now, he was here with a group of men and women. Murph had to say that they all seemed pretty committed. They clearly had put in a long day, especially when one had to consider that the day almost ended before it started during the fiasco with Charles. All in all, Murph felt a combination of emotions. He was sure of one thing though, for the first time he felt like they were finally starting to become a team.

"Coach?" Bea repeated.

"Oh, sorry," Murph said. "I guess I kind of got lost in a thought there for a minute."

"I asked where we were eating supper tonight."

"Oh, at the cafeteria again."

Even the collective groans couldn't dampen Murph's newfound optimism.

After supper ended, Murph invited his team to the "living room" of the dorm. With the students away, the group had the run of the place. Although alcohol was outlawed on campus, a rule Murph had bent on a special occasion here and there, a cooler with some cold adult beverages just happened to show up. It was Murph's way to reward the group for a good job today. It never even dawned on the coach that some people might look unfavorably on the gesture. Fortunately for Murphy, no one like that was in this particular group.

"How in the world did you think of doing this," Denise asked as they all sat around a fireplace in well-worn leather couches and overstuffed chairs.

"Actually, it was my wife who thought of it," Murph said.

"Well, it's a great idea," Bea said. "I haven't felt this good about work in a long, long time."

"Me, too," Dave added. "If you would've told me that

we were going to spend an entire day together in a classroom setting and that I was going to walk away looking forward to doing it again, well, I would've said you were nuts."

"I would actually have to agree with that," Joseph said.

"So, what's the agenda tomorrow?" Marti asked

"We'll start at 8," Murph said. "We'll go through the morning and break for lunch at 11. Then we'll come back and wrap things up."

"Just tell me we're eating somewhere besides the cafeteria again – please?" Bea asked.

"Very funny," Murph snorted. "You know, I ate there every day for an awful lot of years when I worked here."

"Yeah," Bea quipped, "and when you tried to retire, look what happened to you."

Billy broke up the brewing squabble.

"Coach, I'm curious. When you decided to bring us all here, what were you hoping to accomplish?"

"I guess it's a couple of things," Murph started. "First, I think that we weren't getting anywhere with the way things have been going at the plant. You guys know that. That's my job as the leader and I don't think I was doing a very good job of leading. So, it was time to change the plan. By coming here, I really wanted to do what we've already talked about. I wanted to break down what's not working, what is working and why in each case. Today, I think you guys did a great job in breaking everything down. Tomorrow, we'll figure out the whys and the what to do about it."

"What're the other reasons?"

"Vision and Gene Sarazen," Murph answered.

"Huh and who?" Bea asked.

Murph chuckled. "Are any of you golf fans?"

"I play a little," Dave said.

"Know who Gene Sarazen is?" Murph asked.

"He was a pretty famous golfer at one time, but I can't say I know much about him."

COACHING SUCCESS

"Sarazen is the golfer who pretty much made the Masters golf tournament what it is today."

"How?"

"Well, Sarazen hit what was called the shot heard round the world when he recorded a very rare double eagle on the 15th hole of the 1935 Masters," Murph explained.

"What's a double eagle?" Joseph asked.

"It is three shots under par and it's more rare than a hole in one," Murph said. "The thing that Sarazen did was make a double eagle to win the Masters."

"OK," Bea said with a smile, "I'll play your silly little game. What's the lesson in this story?"

"Well, from where Sarazen was in the golf tournament, he had all but lost. However, he had the vision to see victory when no one else could. He had the vision, he took the shot and it paid off."

"Yeah, but you said it was very rare," Denise pointed out. "So, more than anything he just got lucky."

"To a degree," Murph agreed. "But luck or not, you guys all know that not everyone sees the possibilities at our plant. They don't have the vision. Sarazen did. You guys do. Doesn't it just make sense that before anything can be really accomplished, somebody has to have the vision to see it?"

Heads nodded all around.

"OK, you guys got me started, so this is your fault. But I'll add one more thing to this. And this is not a football story."

"Be still my heart," Bea kidded, getting Murph to shake his head in mock disgust.

"Everyone has heard that Babe Ruth, one of the most famous home run hitters in baseball history, also held the record for the most strikeouts. That's pretty well known and the point is that in order to achieve great things, you have to endure some failures. Thomas Edison, for example, attempted about 10,000 different tries while working on the filament inside the light bulb. When he finally succeeded, someone asked him why he hadn't given up during the 10,000 failures. He said he hadn't failed 10,000 times but that he had invented 10,000 ways that would not work.

"But back on baseball. The great Bambino (that's Babe Ruth for your benefit Bea) hit 60 home runs during one season in 1927. That record stood for 34 years until 1961 when Roger Maris and Mickey Mantle both made a real run at it. Turns out, Maris belts 61 homers and takes over the record. However, think about it. It took 34 years before someone broke that record. And in those 34 years, let's just say you've got an average of 24 teams per year and let's just say 30 players who bat per team. That's 720 players each year with a chance to break the record and don't. Over that time frame, that's almost 25,000 guys with a chance to do it and can't, or don't.

"But wait, there's more," Murph said in his TV announcer voice.

"In 1998 Mark McGwire and Sammy Sosa chased each other for the home run record. Now remember, only Babe Ruth and Roger Maris — out of the thousands and thousands who have played the game since it first began — have managed to hit at least 60 home runs in one season. So here comes McGwire and Sosa. Boom! They both break it. McGwire hits 70 and Sosa hits 66. Now guess what? As soon as it's clear that there's nothing magical or mystical about it, it's been done four more times. Go figure that out. In 34 years, only twice can anyone break the 60 barrier. As soon as it happens again, the lid is off the jar and they start popping out. Six times since Maris and Ruth! Six in four seasons. On this hand it was done twice in more than half a century of baseball history and then it's done six times in four seasons."

"So what's the point?" Joseph asked. "I'm missing it."

"The point," Murph went on, "is that as soon as everyone could share in the vision, as soon as they could see that it wasn't some unattainable achievement but instead something they were each capable of doing, then everything changed!

"That's one of the things I want to accomplish here," Murph went on. "I want us to see the vision of how great our company could be. We've been spending all our time the past few months working our tails off trying to make nickel improvements when what we're capable of is million-dollar leaps."

With that, Murph stood and stretched. "Listen, it's late and I'm not as young as I used to be. If you all will excuse me, I'm going to turn in."

Everyone said their good nights and Joseph, Billy and Marti headed up to their own rooms as well.

"I've got to say," Denise started. "I'm really starting to warm up to this guy. I mean he's real, he has great ideas and he pours his heart into it."

"I agree," Bea said. "I want him and us to – as he says – win."

"I don't disagree," Dave said. "But we've still got a long way to go. It's one thing to get all of us fired up while we're here, but doing it day in and day out in that plant is a different story."

"Well duh," Bea shot back. "I think that's what he's teaching us how to do."

The next morning, Murph was up by 5:15 and in Max' office by 6. The stairs didn't seem quite as steep today as they did yesterday.

"So, how'd it go yesterday?" Max asked.

"We're making progress," Murph answered, drawing a loud laugh from Max.

"Man, Coach, how many times did you say that exact same thing in the newspapers?"

"A few," Murph smiled. "But I'll tell you what, Coach, business writers ask lot harder questions than sports writers ever did. I don't know why it's different, but it is.

These business writers don't let me get away with answering their question without really saying anything."

Both old friends sipped their coffee and spent the next 90 minutes doing just that – talking about a whole lot without really saying much. And that was perfectly fine with both of them.

Effie had the room in perfect shape again when the gang arrived. In fact, she had found a broom, a rag and some spray cleaner. Murph, who wasn't a sloppy guy by any stretch, had truly never seen the room look better.

"Good morning, everyone," he started cheerfully. "I trust you all slept well."

"Anyone who talks about the good old days in college doesn't remember how small and uncomfortable dorm beds are," Bea said rubbing her neck. "On the other hand, it was quiet."

"OK, before we really get going this morning, I need to make you all aware of something," Murph said. "I wasn't sure whether I should tell you this morning, or wait until later. But I'm sharing this now because I want to get it out of the way, talk about it if we really need to and then move on.

"I decided that the best thing to do after yesterday's incident with Charles was suspend him for a couple of days. I'm not apologizing for it, but neither am I jumping up and down about it. Any questions?"

"Only suspended?" Bea asked incredulously.

"Yes," Murphy said simply.

Everyone was quiet. Most were surprised at the fact that Charles was indeed just suspended. They were all convinced that he was history after that outburst. The fact that Murph didn't fire him impressed a couple of them. A couple of others thought it made him look weak. Murphy figured as much and had already decided, as he always did, that some things just needed to be left alone. This was one of them.

COACHING SUCCESS

"OK, if nothing else, let's proceed with today's agenda," Murph said opening a folder and passing out papers. "You all remember yesterday when we went through and detailed what we felt was holding us back? Effie was gracious enough to compile all the things we said that she recorded on the flip charts and has printed them out for you.

"But we're going to do it a bit differently today. Instead of standing up here and leading this session on what do we do about those things, I am going to swap places with Bea and she's going to lead us this morning."

> **MURPH'S PLAYBOOK**
>
> *Opening up information is important in pulling teams together. However, some information, especially when it comes to personnel, is important to keep confidential. Not everyone will like this. But it will be difficult for them to disagree with it, or not respect it.*

With that, Murphy tossed the dry erase marker to Bea and plopped on a couch. It was vintage Murphy. Over the years Murph had several assistants who had gone on to head coaching jobs. All of them had plenty of practice leading these sessions. Murphy did it for several reasons. He knew that a coach standing at the front of the room would offer more opinions from a leadership position than from sitting back in the shadows. He also knew that hearing the same voice all the time got old, thus increasing the chances that staleness would lull them to sleep and they might miss something important. He also knew that very few assistant coaches, especially at the smaller colleges, wanted to be assistants forever. If he could help groom them, they'd be ready for the next step when the time came. Did that make him someone who just enjoyed always grooming young coaches? No, not at all. But by establishing a strong cadre of potential head coaches, he tended to hang on to assistants until they did get that head job. It also meant that the best of the up and comers would want to work for Murphy. Like everything Murph did, he knew that the best answer was the one that was "win-win."

"Sure, I'll just take right over," Bea, one never to be bashful, said. "My first decision is that we're going to have lunch someplace besides that awful cafeteria."

"You're not that much in charge," Murph deadpanned from the back. "Just get going."

> **MURPH'S PLAYBOOK**
>
> *Coaches sometimes defer to a team captain or an assistant coach. Sharing the "power" only increases the role of the head coach.*

"Fine. OK, we identified a long list of things that were preventing us from reaching our potential yesterday people. I would look at these like roadblocks. So, let us focus our attention today on ways to either remove these roadblocks or at least find ways around . . ."

She stopped and looked back at Murphy and smiled.

"My apologies people," she smiled. "I think we can look at these 'roadblocks' like big, hulking football guys. Our mission then is to figure out how the heck we run right over them!"

Everyone laughed, including Murphy. "Gosh Bea," he said above the laughter, "I coached for almost 30 years and on your first day you've got that lingo – 'big, hulking football guys' down pat. Way to go!"

"If I had a whistle, I'd blow the, uh, how do you guys say, the dad-gum thing at you," she laughed.

Suddenly, it hit Murph that this was the same give and take he enjoyed so much with Max Petry. Maybe they were making some progress, indeed.

"People, people, let's get serious here or I'm going to have you all out running laps," Bea said in her toughest

COACHING SUCCESS

coach-voice.

"Let's start with rewards and appraisals," she said. "Dave, what can we do about that?"

"We could actually *do* appraisals," he said with a strong emphasis on the word "do."

"Good point," Bea said. "Any idea why we don't, Oscar?"

"I don't know, Bea," he said. "I mean I've been there for more than 30 years and I've never had one."

"Come on people," Bea said. "How hard can this one be? Can't we just decide that we will put in a performance appraisal system now? I mean we can tweak it as we go, but let's get it started."

"Does that mean people won't get their annual raises without one?" Denise asked.

"My people don't now," Billy tossed in. "We give raises in my department to those who earn them."

"Well, it's not that way in my department," Marti said. "If we go back there now and tell everyone that they're not getting a raise this year – "

"Whoa Marti," Bea jumped in. "No one is saying they aren't going to get a raise. No one is saying that at all. But why should someone just get a raise for being there? I mean is there anything in the world wrong with saying you have to earn it?"

No one said anything for a minute. Murph kept quiet on purpose.

"My Daddy used to say that you can never go wrong by doing the right thing," Bea explained. "I would guess that the folks who are not being appraised and who are just getting raises every year feel that's the right thing. But I think we all know it's not. Let's go back and let our folks know that we're going to work with them. Shoot, it's our jobs to help them get better. Will they all be thrilled? No. But it's still the right thing to do."

"I'd say you just flattened that big, hulking football guy," Denise said. "You go girl."

"Before we move on, I just want to go on record as saying I don't think it's a good idea to tie raises to these performance appraisals," Joseph said. "Why couldn't we start the appraisals, but give them a year to adjust before we impact their pay?"

"I like that idea," Marti said.

"Wait a minute," Billy jumped in. "First, we're already doing it. Second, if we do that we're just saying 'go ahead and do a crappy job and we'll give you a raise anyway this year.' What kind of message is that? I have to agree with Bea, this is the right thing and we just need to bite the bullet and move on."

"I hate to agree with Billy," Dave kidded. "But I'm on his and Bea's side. Besides, we would really be de-motivating the ones who are doing a good job."

Everyone was wondering if Murph was going to chime in. He just sat there.

"It sounds like we have some disagreement," Bea said. "You've all raised good points. Coach, what do we do?"

"Why ask me?" Murph said. "You guys are covering all the sides. Bring it to a conclusion."

"Fine," Bea said. "Coach put me in charge so this one's final. We'll just do it."

Everyone sat and stared at her.

"Kidding people! Just kidding," Bea laughed. "Joseph, Marti, you two are the ones who seem to have the biggest issue with this. What do you two think after hearing Billy and Dave?"

"I still don't like it," Joseph said. "We have some people who've been there a long, long time. We can't just change the rules on them in mid-stream."

"I've never understood that," Denise said. "Things change all the time. Why do you think that we can't or shouldn't change the rules in mid-stream? I mean, isn't it better to do that than go out of business and let them all look for new jobs?"

COACHING SUCCESS

"I don't think we're going to go out of business," Joseph answered.

"No?" Denise said. "No offense to Coach Murphy here, but how many different bosses have you had since you've been here, Joseph? I think Smith was pretty plain that he wants this to be a success, but his patience is wearing thin."

"I guess I'll change my mind," Marti said quietly. "I think you're right Denise. My husband had to go through an awful lot of changes in his job. They even laid off a whole lot of people. I think the way I've been looking at is kind of similar to sticking my head in the sand."

> **MURPH'S PLAYBOOK**
>
> *Coaches are not timid to change the game plan in the middle of a game if need be. Why are businesses?*

Bea looked to Murph for some sign, but couldn't detect anything. She took a deep breath. "I don't believe this should be decided by majority rule, Joseph," she started. "But unless you or someone else has some pretty good reasons to drag this out, I think we ought to make this change and move on."

Joseph just nodded.

"OK then, next subject."

When Effie signaled that lunch would be ready in 15 minutes, they weren't even halfway through the list from the day before. What they had done so far had taken a long time.

Murph stood up and walked toward the front. "First off, this was an amazingly productive morning. Maybe we didn't get as far as we wanted, but I think we all need to give Coach Bea here a hand for a great job."

Everyone applauded and Bea did her best bow.

"In honor of Coach Bea's leadership skills, anyone want to have lunch from somewhere other than the cafeteria?"

Every hand in the room shot up at once. Murphy sighed.

"Effie has arranged for sandwiches from that little deli down the street. If it's OK with you guys, we'll eat in here and just keep on going?"

"Oh man is that fine with us!" Bea said. "I think we're willing to work all through the night if we don't have to eat again in that cafeteria."

"Sheesh," Murph sighed. "OK, Coach Bea, how about you finishing up your assignment? After you wrap up, Billy you take over for this afternoon's session, OK?"

Time flew for the rest of the day. The group decided to implement an employee recognition system by delegating the assignment to what Murphy called Impact Teams. The assignment would be to create a system that would recognize as much good work as possible. The senior staff really believed Murph's idea that good teams were good not only because they were skilled, but also because they "thought" they were good. A "swagger" Murphy called it. They all wanted their teams to walk with a swagger. They also decided to conduct weekly training programs. Like Murphy's Huskies teams, their team would only get better with constant practice. They also decided to add a suggestion box. But the biggest idea the group came up with was one that

> **MURPH'S PLAYBOOK**
>
> *Sports teams practice routinely. Yet in business, training can be viewed as an expense, or a luxury. Think of it in terms of skills. If a sports team practices two hours a day, four days a week, that's eight hours to hone the skills that make it successful. How can businesses* not afford to *spend regular time on training?*

COACHING SUCCESS

Murph figured he had to go see Walt Smith about.

With Billy leading the group on how they could continue and enhance what they were already doing right, they came up with the basic outline of a profit sharing plan. The idea was essentially to take all the profits beyond a certain mark and split them with the employees 50-50. For example, for every dollar that they earned beyond the goal, 50 cents would go to the company and 50 cents would go into an employee pool. Full-timers would get a full share and part-timers would get a half share. Murph loved the idea, but told the group he would have to get Walt to sign off before he could move forward on that one.

By the time 5 o'clock rolled around, the group was exhausted, but excited. Murph's plan from the beginning had been to give them all Friday off so they could go home and catch up on their rest. That way they could come in Monday raring to go. However, no one would take him up on the offer. They were all ready to get back and get going with these new plans.

Driving home, Murph had mixed emotions. On one hand, Murph was more excited than at any other time since he had started. On the other hand, he knew that tomorrow would bring him face to face with Charles. Effie told him that Charles had been instructed to show up at 9 a.m. for a meeting with Murph. Although Murphy was willing to give Charles a chance to come back, he knew at some level inside that it wasn't going to happen. Charles had made up his mind long before Murphy came along that he was always going to be unhappy. Murph couldn't understand it. He had seen other people with the same traits. Why would anyone want to give that much control of their own emotions to other people or other sources? If an event or a person can make someone miserable, didn't it really make sense that the miserable person had given that event or that person the ability to make them feel that way? Although the logic of that made sense to Murphy, the idea of allowing it to happen was absolutely foreign to him.

Murphy couldn't remember the details, but he had heard a story about a prisoner of war in who had decided to be happy. His decision was spurred by the fact that he wasn't going to let his captors force him to be unhappy. His mind was the one area they couldn't touch and he was determined not to give that up.

Although Murphy didn't know any other details, he thought it was a powerful story. If a man in the worst possible conditions could decide to remain happy, how could someone let a simple job poison his or her outlook?

As he pulled the Jeep into his drive, Murph suddenly realized how much he missed his wife. It had been a couple of days since he had seen her. Usually when he spent the night in the film room, he was dragging by the time he got home from a lack of sleep. However, he had gotten plenty of rest and decided as he walked up the sidewalk that he would take his lovely bride to her favorite restaurant tonight.

But when he opened the door, the smell of his favorite dinner – Shepherd's Pie – greeted him in full force. Charles or not, Murph once again thought he must truly be the luckiest guy on the planet.

The next morning found Murph at the plant bright and early as usual. Although he was not looking forward to this one on one with Charles, he had been through it before. He had a young coach years ago that stretched the truth a little when he was talking to recruits. That was something Murphy just couldn't tolerate. There were a few others over the years, although not nearly as many as other schools had. It was a fact that Murphy was proud of. Although his coaching staff had its share of turnover, it was almost always caused when one of his assistant coaches got an opportunity to move up the ranks. In the coaching world, being an assistant under Coach Murphy meant that you were going to work hard, learn a lot and be groomed. Young guys knew it was only a matter of time before they would get a shot at a head coaching job.

At 8:45 his intercom buzzed and Effie announced that Charles was there.

Murph looked at his watch and checked it against the wall clock. Was he really there 15 minutes early? Maybe this was a good sign?

Charles came through the door and walked straight to Murphy's desk, stopping quickly and throwing the suspension letter he had received at Murphy. "Who the hell do you think you are to suspend me?" Charles started out loudly. "I've put in 42 years and I've been a loyal employee. I've given 42 years of my life to this place, you son of a bitch. Who do you think you are?"

"Charles, please, sit down and let's talk this through before we have nothing left to talk about," Murph said as evenly as he could manage. He looked Charles straight in the eye and didn't look away. After a moment or two, Charles stepped back and took a seat.

"So, I guess you figure you're going to fire me and be done with it," Charles said. "Well, let me tell you something mister. If you want to make that mistake, you go right ahead. First off, my department would fall apart if I weren't there to run it. And second off, I'll sue your ass for wrongful termination and for age discrimination. I'll own this place before the day is out."

"Charles, I've not decided to fire you, so let's back off a little, OK?" Murphy said. "Where this goes is absolutely up to you."

Murphy sighed inwardly and leaned forward, putting his hands palm down on the desk. "Charles, it seems like we've been in this position once before, and I think I told you the same thing then. I meant it then and I mean it now. There's one big difference this time, though. While it's still your decision, my tolerance and patience are wearing thin."

"Your tolerance!" Charles practically screamed. "You just walked in as the new boss. You haven't spent years watching and working for others who you knew weren't as good as you. You want to talk about tolerance? I can teach a course on tolerance."

Murphy wanted to come out of his chair and tell this arrogant egomaniac a thing or two, but giving in to his emotions wasn't going to do he or Charles any good. Murph didn't believe you should never show emotions, even anger. He just believed you should do it in a controlled way. A coach Murph played for when he was a kid told him that when Murph got his first coaching job. He said it was OK to yell at a player. Just make sure to do it for effect, not out of anger. If Murph gave in to his emotions right now, it would be out of anger.

"Listen Charles," Murph started. "You and I are in a similar position on at least one thing."

"I doubt that," Charles shot back.

"Really, we are," Murph said calmly. "Neither one of us wants to be here right now. From where I sit, it looks to me like I'm awfully close to losing a member of senior staff and I don't want that. Charles, I'd really like to find a way to work this out, but if we do, there are some things that absolutely have to change."

For a moment, there was only silence. However, Murphy knew that if there was any chance at all for this to work out with Charles still a member of the company, then he'd have to get some changes agreed to between the two of them.

Finally, Charles leaned forward. "I'm listening."

"This constant, I don't know how else to say it, being a thorn in my side, has to stop. Charles, if you want to hate me, that's up to you. I honestly don't know what you base it on since we really don't know each other all that well. But, how you feel about me is absolutely your call. However, how you treat others and me around the company is my call. And if you want to continue working here, then that has to change."

To his credit, Charles didn't argue what he knew to be a valid point. In fact, he didn't argue, or even speak for a full minute. The silence this time went so long that Murphy was starting to get a little uncomfortable.

"And if I don't?" Charles asked.

"Then we're going to be done," Murphy said.

Charles shook his head. The look on his face struck Murphy as odd. It was part anger and part worry.

"You fire me and you know I'm going to sue this place," Charles said with a slight shake in his voice.

"That's certainly up to you," Murph said. "I was hoping that we could find a better answer."

"Like what?"

"Well, first I'd like to find common ground where we can work together. If not, I talked to Walt this weekend and we both agree that if this is going to end that we don't want it to end this way," Murph said. "We feel like you have given a lot of your life to this company and we are willing to offer you an early retirement package that I believe you'll find more than fair. All the documents are in this," he said opening a drawer and handing Charles a large sealed envelope.

"The accountants and lawyers say that you should spend a couple of days looking them over and you can certainly have your own lawyer review them. If you find anything we should talk over, give me a call and we'll talk. If you agree with the terms, then we'll cut you a check and start the benefits."

For a minute, Charles just stared at Murphy. Then he looked down and opened the envelope. Murphy could see his eyes widen just a bit as he looked at the first couple of lines of the generous offer.

"Why, why would you do this?" Charles asked, still looking into the envelope.

"Because it's not about winning and losing, Charles. It's about fairness and it's about finding a way for everyone involved to feel good about it. Look, Charles, am I happy about the way you've been since I got here? No, no I'm not. However, parting ways probably is the best answer for everyone involved, even if you and I don't want to admit that. With the amount of time you have invested here, it just makes sense to make this parting as painless as possible."

Again, Charles just sat there and didn't say anything. After what seemed like forever to Murphy, Charles slowly stood and looked down at Murphy.

"Well, you can bet I'll have my lawyer go over this and if you are trying to screw me, I'll make your life miserable." With that, he turned and walked out, leaving the door open as he went through it.

"I wouldn't expect anything different," Murph said to no one.

Murphy was a little surprised that the buzz around the plant concerning Charles was exactly like the buzz around a team when a player left under adverse circumstances. For a few days it seemed to dominate water cooler conversations. Then it began to die off. In both cases, the majority of the team / plant seemed to understand that it was for the best and life went on. Murph thought it might have been Mark Twain who once said something about never answering criticism. Something about your friends didn't need it and your enemies would never believe it. This whole incident just reaffirmed that philosophy.

After a couple of days, Charles had indeed returned the signed agreement that paid him a portion of his pay for each year served. It also gave him a deal on his insurance for the near term until he reached the proper age so that wouldn't be a concern or burden to Charles and his family. And at that age, his regular pension would also kick in. In short, Charles came out smelling like a rose. The only two things he had to do was not go into competition against the company and keep his mouth shut about the deal. Murphy knew the first part wouldn't be a problem — mainly because the company didn't really have much competition to speak of in the area. But Murph knew the second part had to be driving Charles crazy. There was another old saying Murph liked, although he didn't have any idea who said it. Maybe it was from a fortune cookie, but it was something about the best revenge being to live well. He really wished for Charles that the guy would find a way to let go of his hate and animosity and just learn to live well.

Murphy also had to deal with some issues on the senior staff. A couple of them had come to see Murphy about Charles. They had started off by saying that they could understand Murphy's frustration with Charles. Everyone felt that way at times about the guy. But, they reasoned, Charles had more than 40 years with the company. Maybe it would be nice for Murphy to reconsider and let Charles come back?

When Murphy explained that the decision had been Charles', and that the company had offered him a generous severance package, that was good enough for two of them. Bea, however, looked at Murphy and said she thought the company had paid the guy to do nothing for at least the last 10 years and she didn't understand why he ought to have anything else coming to him. Then she thanked Murphy for his time and for letting her get that off her chest and left. In spite of himself, Murphy had to smile. He absolutely knew that if he ever needed a completely honest answer, Bea was the one to go to.

So as the buzz around the plant died down, life did anything but return to normal. The remaining senior staff was seeing to that. All departments were going through a major metamorphosis. Training wasn't just something that was either talked about or was done once a year. Training was now an ongoing part of the process.

Tim Timmons

As Murph walked around the plant he saw posters – some handmade, some professionally done – that showed any number of things. Some showed a department's progress on its goals. Some showed employees who had done something special. He even saw one outside a department that just had five employees pictured. Three were having birthdays that month and two were celebrating anniversaries (Murph made a note in the daily planner he carried everywhere so that he could pop in on those days and give a personal greeting). He even saw a poster entitled "Keys to Victory." It had five points:
  1. Play to win
  2. Be fair to employees, customers and company
  3. Share and focus
  4. Reward achievements – respect efforts
  5. Active accountability

Although he knew the five points by heart, it made him feel a little good to see them on the wall. At least he was getting through to some of them.

Another thing that shouldn't have been a big surprise to Murphy was the monthly results. The first month after the sessions in the film room was what Murph called a win. The plant met its budget expectations. The afternoon when Murph got the report, he couldn't quit grinning. He asked Effie to call the senior staff members to his office for a five-minute impromptu meeting.

When they had all arrived a few minutes later, Murph looked serious.

"A few weeks ago, we talked about our "record." At the time we were 0-2, meaning we had missed our budget the first two months of the year. Our goal, we all agreed, was to go 10-0 for the remaining 10 months of this year – quite an ambitious goal since we were 3-9 in the 12 months prior. Does everyone remember that?"

Heads nodded.

"Good, because I wanted to tell you that we are, right

now, officially 1-2. We made our month!"

A loud chorus of cheers erupted from the group. High fives were exchanged and Murphy had to smile. It really did look a lot like a locker room at that moment.

"Great work to all!" Murph said above the din. "Now, we've been posting our monthly reports outside the conference room so everyone could have a chance to go by and see exactly how we're doing. On this one though, how do we let everyone in the building know the good news quicker?"

"We have a plant-wide meeting, our second, scheduled for next week anyway, let's tell them then," Billy suggested.

"No, that's too long," Bea said.

"Yeah," Denise added. "We need to tell them now."

"I don't see what waiting a few days will do," Joseph said. "I believe it will be perfectly fine to wait until our regularly scheduled meeting to share the results with them – although I still have great misgivings about sharing the actual numbers."

"Noted, Joseph," Murph acknowledged. "But I agree with Bea and Denise. I think we need to share this now. I mean look at you guys. You're all whooping and hollering and feeling good. This is a great accomplishment and we need to share the information *as well as* the enthusiasm."

"Hey," Marti exclaimed. "How about the dollar theater down the street? They don't show any movies during the mornings there and we could get everyone in. They even have a stage from back in the days when it was a community theater. We could get everyone in and it could be a cool way to make an announcement like this."

"I'd hate to pull everyone off the lines and all their jobs – seriously hurting our numbers for that day and endangering this month – just so we can tell them they made last month," Oscar tossed in. "I mean this is really good news, but in the end, it's only one month. When we go 10-0, then we pull everyone together."

"Agreed, Oscar," Murph said. "How about this? One of our goals was to create a company newsletter of some sort. Let's put out our first issue as an "extra" like the old newspapers used to do with big news. We can distribute it tomorrow."

"That's great," Dave said. "But who's going to get it all done in one day?"

"Don't worry," Murph smiled, pushing a button on the intercom. "I just happen to know someone who is an incredibly talented, giving, generous professional and in need of an extra vacation day.

"Oh Effie, want to make a deal?"

Chapter 8

The next four months flew past, the same way a successful season used to feel. At just past the halfway point of the year, the plant had a 5-2 record and for the first time in anyone's memory – including Walt Smith's – the plant had hit budget for five straight months. If Murph had any doubters in the plant, they were dwindling quickly. Plus, the five months left in the year looked to be the best months of the whole year. It didn't hurt that those same five months from the previous year weren't very good. That was helpful since the budget was based on actual results from the prior year. It also meant that Murph & Co. had a legitimate chance of doing what seemed impossible just a few months ago.

Things were changing. They were changing all over, but especially in Charles' former department. Murphy had spent a fair amount of time there after Charles had left. He noticed an immediate change the first time he walked in. A bright floral arrangement was just inside the door.

"What's this?" he asked, bending over to take a whiff.

"Oh sorry, sir," the lady sitting at the nearby desk had said. "I'll get rid of them right away."

"Nonsense," Murph said. "They make the place look brighter and they smell good. I was just wondering if someone had a birthday or something?"

"No sir," she said quietly. "I brought them from home."

"Home?" Murph asked. "You grow these?"

"Yes sir."

"Well, this looks great. Have you ever brought flowers in before?"

"No sir."

"Why not? These are beautiful."

"Mr. Jones didn't like them and said it was inappropriate. I'm sorry if I've said something wrong, sir."

Murphy felt his neck getting warm. Not only was this woman never allowed to brighten her workplace, and her day, with her own flowers, but it was clear from her subservient manner that she was used to being put down.

"Well, I'll tell you what . . . Cheryl," Murph said looking at her badge. "I think these flowers look lovely. In fact, they're so lovely, I'd appreciate two things from you."

"Yes sir?"

"I'd appreciate it if you would quit calling me 'sir,' first of all. And second, if you ever have any spare flowers you want to bring in, I'd be honored to see them in our lobby."

Murph smelled the flowers one last time, smiled at Cheryl and walked away. He couldn't tell which was brighter, the arrangement or Cheryl's new-found smile.

All through the department, Murphy found people who looked like they were just awakening from a long nap. Some were at first afraid to speak up or say much. Of course there were also some others who had learned well, too well, from Charles. Those would have to learn to change, Murphy thought. If not, well then they certainly didn't have good observation powers. However, this whole area was being merged into Bea's department and Murph figured if anyone could reach these people, Bea could.

There just wasn't any question in Murph's mind that

COACHING SUCCESS

Bea was the best of the best on his senior staff. When Murph pulled everyone together to discuss the hiring a replacement, Bea had been the first to suggest that they examine other options. Bea's point, Murph remembered, was that if they needed a replacement then the extra research would help them understand what they should look for. But a thorough look at the existing structure might show that a new strategy might be in order. Coming from someone else, Murph might have suspected an ulterior motive. But from Bea, it just made sense. So when the group – a group that did not include Bea – concluded that the work being done closely intertwined with Bea's area, well, it all just made sense.

The actual change was going to take place in the next few days. Not only was Murph pretty confident that it would work, he strongly suspected there would be more flowers and more smiles around this area in the not too distant future.

In fact, things were going so well that a local newspaper wanted to do a story on Murphy. It was a part of the job, the same as it was when he was coaching, that he absolutely hated. He always felt that a coach got way too much credit for a team's success as well as too much blame for their failures. He remembered a good friend who had gotten fired after his team lost the big game against the archrivals. Never mind that the arch rivals were a whole lot better. Never mind that his friend's team actually played over their heads and had a chance to win. They didn't win because a 19-year-old kid missed a 30-something yard field goal. Coaches knew that just getting a team into that position was the ultimate job a coach could do. The fact that the kid missed the kick shouldn't be held against the coach. Heck, it shouldn't be held against the kid, who was just a freshman. It wasn't the pros. Kids made mistakes. But, Murph guessed, maybe it's better that the coach gets blamed instead of the kid. However, today's interview wasn't about blame, it was about credit. And Murph just wanted to make sure that the credit was spread around to all the people it belonged to and not just on him.

"Mr. Murphy, I really appreciate you taking the time to speak with me," the reporter said. The guy was about 50, with graying hair and was tall and thin. He wore glasses, although he kept perching them just above his eyes on his forehead when he looked down at his notebook. Murph had agreed to speak with him after his old pal from the sports department vouched for the guy.

"No problem, Mr. Monigham," Murphy said warmly.

"As you know, my paper is doing a story on how a football coach goes from X's and O's to CEO and, well, you've got to admit, it is pretty amazing."

"Amazes me every day," Murph laughed. "If somebody would've told me I'd be doing this three or four years ago I would've laughed them out of my locker room. However, I've got to say that I wouldn't be here even today if it wasn't for some incredibly talented and dedicated people here in the plant. They actually do all the work."

"Just how did you end up in this job, Mr. Murphy," the reporter asked and began taking notes.

About half an hour into the interview, there was a soft knock on Murph's door. It struck him as odd because he couldn't remember Effie ever knocking on that door since he had been here. She usually either stuck her head in since the door was almost always open, or she buzzed him on the intercom. Even though the door was open even now, Murph could see that Effie had reached around the corner and knocked.

"Hey Effie," Murph said. "What do you need?"

"I'm very sorry to interrupt," she said. Something was wrong. When a stranger was around, Effie put on this super-professional voice that Murphy always kidded her about later. This time, she didn't do that, but she didn't sound like herself either.

"Could I see you out here for a moment?" she asked.

Murphy excused himself and went out the door. As he got closer, he could see that Effie had been crying.

"What's the matter?" Murph asked. "Are you OK?"

"It's Joseph," Effie said in a small voice. "He was coming back from lunch . . ."

Her voice cracked and she brought the tissue up to her face.

"It's OK," Murph said. "Take your time."

"A big truck hit him in the intersection by the ice cream place."

"Oh jeez," Murph said. "Is he OK?"

"No," she said, stifling a sob. "He didn't even make it to the hospital. They said there was nothing anyone could have done."

Murphy's thoughts became a blur. He had just seen Joseph that morning. Now he was gone. What about . . .

"His wife," Murph blurted out. "Has she been told? Is she OK? Of course she's not OK. Does she know?"

"Yes, she's on the way to the hospital. I guess that's where they take . . ."

Effie started crying. Murph gave her a hug and was more than a little choked up himself. "We need to let his folks know, and we need to let the plant know, too," Murph said. "Are you going to be alright?"

Effie smiled a little and dabbed at her eyes with a tissue. "You know me, Coach. I'll get it done."

"I know you will, Effie. Thank you! Do you need a few minutes?"

"Let me go to the little girls' room and get my face fixed," she said. "I'll hold it together."

Murph walked back into his office. "Mr. Monigham, I'm sorry, but something has just come up and I need to cut this short."

"Nothing bad, I trust," the reporter said.

Murph was somewhat stuck. His past experience told

him that if he said he couldn't say that would be like throwing a piece of meat into the water with alligators. They'd thrash about until they got it. On the other hand, there was no way he was telling this guy what just happened. He didn't want any of Joseph's family or friends hearing about this through the media.

"It's not something I can go in to at this moment," Murph said. "But if you'll bear with me on this, I promise I'll give you a call before the end of the day today. Fair enough?"

The reporter was puzzled, but at the same time didn't really see any alternatives. He figured it was likely a broken piece of equipment or something like that. He agreed and the two shook hands and left. Murph immediately went over to his desk and picked the phone up. The local chief of police was a big Huskies booster and Murphy knew him well. He figured if he could reach the guy that he'd get all the information he'd need.

Thirty minutes later, Murphy had already informed the senior staff and had had a quick meeting with Joseph's staff. He had reached Walt Smith. Everyone took it hard. Although no one really liked Joseph all that much, he was still part of the team and his death was an absolute shock. Afterward, Murphy made the announcement over the public address system in the plant. Finally, Murphy picked up the phone and called the paper. He asked for Monigham.

"Business, Monigham," the voice on the other end said.

"Mr. Monigham, T.J. Murphy," he started.

"Mr. Murphy, I'm so sorry. I heard after I got back to the paper."

"Thanks," Murphy said. "You understand that I couldn't say anything?"

"Absolutely. Listen, you take care of what you need to do and I'll get back to you in a week or so."

Murphy, unfortunately, was stunned. He wasn't used

to reporters being this understanding, or this nice. "That's very kind of you," Murph said. "I could call you next week sometime."

"Listen Mr. Murphy, there are some things that are just more important than a story. You just let me know when's a good time after all this is over and we'll go from there."

"Thank you Mr. Monigham," Murph said. "I promise I'll get back to you."

Murph hung the phone up. He didn't know if the reporter realized or even cared, but he had just made a friend for life.

The funeral was three days later. From a business standpoint, the timing could not have been worse. The plant had already suffered a couple of setbacks during the month and there were serious doubts as to whether or not a sixth-straight "win" was in the cards. In the days after Joseph's accident, productivity fell through the floor and the month was in serious jeopardy. Still, Murph had to make a decision about the funeral. Should they close the plant for the afternoon so that everyone who wanted to go could? Or should they try and keep the operations going and just let those who wanted to go off for a couple of hours? Murph didn't talk it over with senior staff, in part because he felt strongly that they didn't get paid enough to have to make these kinds of decision. This one was up to him.

In the end, it really wasn't a decision. Murph felt that the right thing to do was close the plant that afternoon and let everyone have a chance to attend the funeral. He called the senior staff to set the wheels in motion.

"Whoa, wait a minute," Billy said. "I mean I don't want to show any disrespect to Joseph or anything, but I don't think we need to close the whole place down. If we do that, there's no way we'll hit our month. That will cost people shots at bonuses. It will throw us way behind. In my department, it will be devastating on morale."

"Oh crap, Billy," Bea said. "It'll be a bigger boot to morale if we keep working while they bury Joseph."

"Look, I don't want to sound cold or anything here," Billy said. "But the truth of the matter is that Joseph had the kind of personality that didn't necessarily make people warm up to him. I don't think that many people here really felt like they knew him. And in my department, we actually have a string of 14 straight months of hitting our numbers. If we shut down for even an afternoon, I think that'll be gone."

Murph sighed. The only thing bigger than Billy's talents was his ego. And it bothered Murphy as a person when he saw someone act that way.

"I appreciate what you're all saying," Murph said. "But this is just one of those things that's my call and we're going to shut down. If it causes us to miss the month, then it does."

The announcement was typed up and given to each employee that afternoon. The note simply said that the right thing to do was to give everyone who wanted to go to the funeral the opportunity to do so. Whether or not anyone did was entirely up to each person. The plant would re-open the next morning as usual.

MURPH'S PLAYBOOK

When in doubt, do the right thing. Sadly, this may not seem to be as true in big college athletics, but it is certainly true in small colleges. And it should certainly be true in anything.

The afternoon of the funeral was a beautiful day. The sky was blue and the sun was shining brightly. It wasn't too hot or too cold. Murphy and Julie, Walt Smith and his wife and all the senior staff and their spouses were all there, except for Billy. Actually, as

COACHING SUCCESS

Murph looked around at the overflow crowd, he could see that if the whole plant didn't show up, darn near all of them did. Joseph's wife was particularly moved and went out of her way to thank Murphy and Smith for allowing so many people to come.

For his part, Walt Smith hadn't even raised an eyebrow when Murphy told him of the decision to shut down. In fact, he would've been surprised had Murphy not done so.

When the service finally ended, as is always the case in these situations, everyone was relieved to be on their way. But what happened next was something that would be talked about for years to come.

Murph was especially quiet on the drive home and Julie let her husband be alone with his thoughts. When they got home, Murph leaned over and kissed her on the cheek.

"I know," Julie said. "You just need to run by the plant to do a couple of things."

"You're the best," he said. "I just want to see if there's any way we can pull this month out. Maybe I've missed something. I don't know, I just want to do a little more thinking before I call it a day."

"Sweetheart," she said. "You've done amazing things so far. Letting everyone go to the funeral was the right thing to do. Don't worry about this one month. The bigger picture was more important and you did the right thing."

"I know, I know," he said. "I'm really not worried about it. This was the right thing, and I'd do it all again – God forbid. But maybe it doesn't have to be either or. Maybe there's a way to still make our numbers. If there is a way and I missed it, and it ends up costing people a bonus, I'll never forgive myself."

Julie patted her husband's cheek and got out of the car. She walked to the front door and wished that the people in the plant could see how much Murph cared. It wasn't that he was ready to move on after seeing Joseph buried. It was the contrary. His responsibility was to show respect to Joseph and his family, which he did in an amazing way. There was no way that many people would've turned out for the funeral if not for Murph. Julie knew that the huge crowd would be a comfort to the Cox family. But now he felt a responsibility to everyone at the plant and he wouldn't rest until he either found an answer or ran himself ragged trying.

When Murph pulled into the parking lot, he was amazed at what he saw. He expected to see a mostly empty lot. Instead, it looked like a normal workday. Cars were everywhere. Some people were just getting out and walking toward the plant. Murph just stared. The more he looked, the less he understood. Why did so many people come back by the plant after the funeral?

Bea saw Murph pull up in his Jeep. She sighed, hoping he wasn't going to be angry. This was the first thing she or any of the department heads had ever done without his full knowledge or blessing. Oh well, she thought, might as well face the music now and get it over with.

"Hey Coach," Bea said as she walked up to Murph.

"Bea, what are all these people . . . who . . . what are you doing here?"

"Well coach, remember a long time ago when you told us that story about the quarterback who changed your play? You said he told you it was a lot easier to ask for forgiveness than permission."

"Yeah, I remember," Murph said.

"Well, then I guess I'm asking for some forgiveness here."

"You?" Murph said, still puzzled. "What's going on?"

"Well, a lot of people were talking about your decision to shut everything down for the funeral," Bea started explaining. "I didn't hear one person, outside of Billy, who disagreed or thought it was the wrong call. But, and this wasn't just my idea or any one person, but a lot of people thought that we could sort of do both. The plan was to go to the funeral and then to come back here and put in some extra hours.

"Coach, you have no idea how badly everyone wants to make this month. We've got five straight and five left to go. Everyone knows that this is the toughest one we have left. No one who works here wants to lose this one. They've all worked too hard the past five months. They've watched how hard you've worked the past five months. Coach, they don't want to let you down. And even more importantly, they don't want to let themselves down."

"Bea, I don't know what to say," Murph said.

"Everyone thought you wouldn't find out about this until tomorrow morning," Bea smiled. "Since you're here now, I guess maybe we ought to get inside and get to work? We wouldn't want to let everyone feel like we're not holding up our end now, would we?"

When Murph walked in, the first thing he did was start walking around the various areas of the plant, shaking hands and saying thank you.

"No problem, Coach, I wouldn't have missed this," was one reply.

"My pleasure, Coach, thanks for saying thanks," said a woman.

"Coach, there's just no way we're going to lose this month," came another.

By the time Murph got to his office, 90 minutes had passed from the moment he walked in the door. He picked up the phone and called his wife and let her know he would be a while. On the other end of the phone, Julie couldn't recall a time when Murph had sounded more emotional.

When the final numbers came in early the next month, Murph flipped through the first couple of pages to get to the bottom line. When he saw it, he immediately turned to his phone and hit the button for the P.A. system.

"If I could have your attention please," Murph said, feeling just as uncomfortable as he always did talking into his phone and having it broadcast over the entire building. Murph waited a couple of seconds. "I just wanted you all to know that you did it. We're officially 6-2 and I don't know of any team anywhere who ever worked harder for a win. Congratulations and thank you all!"

Chapter 9

The only real question left was what to do about Joseph's department. Walt Smith had offered to help with the interviewing if Murph wanted. While he appreciated the offer, Murph had another idea. The first couple of weeks after Joseph's accident, everyone was so busy with just trying to make the month that there wasn't much time spent on hiring. With a new month started, Murph wasn't quite ready to jump into the hiring process. Actually, he wasn't even sure he was going to. He had learned a lesson from the previous situation with Charles. This would be much the same, he decided. In fact, it wasn't terribly different from several times in his past when an assistant coach left to take a head coaching job. Murph took the time to evaluate his and the teams' needs. If it was a linebacker coach, the first question Murph always asked was, did he need a coach for the linebackers? If the answer was yes, he started looking for one. If the answer was no, then the next question was what did he and the team need? That particular team might actually need more help in the secondary, or on the offensive line.

With that in mind, Murph asked Effie to put together a brown bag lunch for Murph and all the members of Joseph's department.

Tim Timmons

Brown bag lunches were something Murph had started when he first came to the plant. Actually, it was something he started many, many years before when he realized it was a good way to deal with some of the more avid boosters. One day a month he would open the locker room for a brown bag lunch for anyone who wanted to show up. Players rarely did because they felt they got to see enough of their coach without an extra lunch tossed in. But boosters and some of the school staff usually came out in droves.

The idea would be to have a nice informal lunch. The staff would set up some training tables and chairs so everyone would have a place to sit and eat. Murphy would usually try to make his way around the room and talk with lots of people and then toward the end he would stand on a bench and say a word or two. It was just another one of the things the coach did that endeared him to the community.

Effie had set aside one of the conference rooms for today's brown bag lunch. Joseph's old department only had a dozen or so staff members, so they didn't need a large area. Murph, as usual, really did have a brown bag. Inside, there was a peanut butter and jelly sandwich, his favorite, and an orange. Murph usually got a cold bottle of milk out of the vending machine.

"Thanks for getting together today," Murph started out after he had finished his sandwich and some small talk on how things were going. "I want to ask you guys a few questions and share with you where things are regarding this department. Let's start out with the second item first.

"The decision I face is what to do about a replacement for Joseph," Murph started out. "But before we go too far along in that decision, I wanted to hear from you guys what you think. We certainly have some experience in thinking a little differently after what we did in merging those two departments under Bea. If we decide that the right thing to do is hire a replacement, then when we get to that point, I would like for all of you to get a chance to meet any candidates during the interview process. What I mean for now is, does it make sense to just make a hire and go back to status quo? Joseph had been in this job for a long time. Has the department changed? Have the requirements of the job changed? Have things evolved to make this different? In short, I want your feedback because you guys are on the front lines and know better than anyone. If you were running this place, what would you do?"

A few months ago, no one would've said anything. Even today, the people who worked in Joseph's department weren't quite as open and receptive as say the people in Bea's area, but they had opened up some the past couple of weeks. Certainly, no one was jumping up to get her or his opinion in first. Murph did notice that a lot of people were looking toward a young woman.

"Melissa, got any ideas?" Murph asked.

The young lady had only worked at the plant for a year or so. All this talk about being a team and working together had probably been more exciting to her than most of the others in the department. She has gone to college on a volleyball scholarship and understood the concepts of winning and losing and of teamwork very well.

"I'm not sure, if it was my decision, that I would keep this department intact," she said, evenly, if not boldly.

"What would you do?" Murph asked, encouraged by this young woman's candor.

"Well, some of the work we do now can be done with software. And I don't mean proprietary stuff. There're some simple off-the-shelf programs that will handle some of the reports we generate. And if we had some of the busy work out of the way, we could work closer with some of the research people to come up with things that might either save the company some money or find ways to grow the company. And if we did that, I mean, wouldn't that be better all around?"

Murph was watching the reaction of the others while this young lady spoke. In effect, she was suggesting turning their entire world upside down. If the idea had no merit, surely a few of them would be ready to say something. Yet most of them were nodding their heads while she talked.

"It sure sounds like that would be better," Murph answered. "Would you be willing to take part in a task force to take a closer look at that concept?" he asked.

She nodded.

"Great," he said. "How about anyone else? Any other ideas or things we ought to be thinking about?"

No one said anything.

"OK, we'll set up a task force," Murph said. "Any of you are welcome to take part in it. The idea will be to create an agenda and a timeline that we all agree is reasonable to make a recommendation on where we go from here. I don't want to rush the group into making a hasty recommendation, but neither do I want to wait a few months before we figure this out either."

With that, Murph thanked everyone again for coming and headed back to get this idea organized.

Effie was waiting for Murph when he got back from the meeting.

"So why is it, Boss, that you want to take the time to form a task force on whether or not we should hire a member of senior staff, but you don't take the time with the person off the front line?" she asked.

"What do you mean," Murph said almost defensively. "I take a lot of time for the folks on the front line."

"I don't mean *with* them," Effie said. "I mean the hiring process."

"Effie, you're going to have to speak English again. You've lost me."

"The hire," she said. "Why don't you spend as much

time on the overall hiring process as you are on this one? I mean I know it's a higher paid position and all. But have you looked at our turnover rates? They're better now than they were, but the cost of turnover is one of the things that have hurt us."

Murphy shook his head. "I understand that," he said. "But what am I missing?"

"First off, you're asking the right questions on this job," she said, reversing the roles of teacher-student once again. "So why don't we do that on every job?"

Before Murph could even answer, Effie just kept on going. "Sure, HR handles a lot of the hiring process, but have you ever sat through any of the interviews? I have. I had to take notes a couple of times. Our folks do all the talking. I don't know how they can decide who the best candidate is that way. I heard you say that the good Lord gave us two ears and one mouth and that ought to tell most folks something."

Murph wasn't sure what to say. He had made a few hires in his lifetime, but it wasn't something he had to do that often. And for better or worse, in the coaching fraternity, hires were made more on the recommendations of other coaches. Murph didn't have any long relationships with other folks in the business world that he could rely on like that.

"So what are you suggesting?" he asked Effie, always willing and eager to be the student with her – or anyone else who was making sense.

"Examine our hiring process overall, not just for a senior position," she answered. "You've taught us all a lot of valuable lessons. Teach us how to make better selections when we hire. Teach us how to decide if we need to replace a person or change the job. Do what you've done all along."

"What I've taught so far are the things I know," Murph said. "You're talking now about a specific set of skills or knowledge that I don't possess. I don't disagree with what you're saying, but I'm not sure what I could do about it.

"What do you think?"

Effie smiled and turned away. "Dunno Coach, that's why you get paid the big bucks!"

Murph almost threw a foam football he kept in his office at her. It wouldn't have been the first time. But she was already out the door before he could've gotten the pass off. Instead, he plopped into his chair. Effie was right. This task force was fine and probably a good idea. But it was only a start. There was a much bigger issue here, and Murph was kicking himself for not seeing it before. He was also kicking himself for not knowing what to do to make it better.

He thought back to coaching. That was part of the problem. In coaching, after so many years, everything was second nature. He didn't run across problems where he felt lost. He wondered what he would've done if he had – then it hit him. Early in his career, one of the pro coaches had come up with a new offense. Although it wasn't at all unusual for a coach to add a wrinkle or two to their existing offensive schemes, this guy had a whole new concept – and was using it to average about 50 points a game. When Murph actually had a chance to see it on film, he liked what he saw. The first thing he did was pick up the phone and call the coach and asked him if they could talk. As long as coaches aren't competing against each other, and even sometimes if they are, they're pretty willing to share information. So, Murph had learned a whole lot of new tricks that summer.

That meant all he had to do was find an expert in this particular area and do some learning.

Chapter 10

Two weeks later, the senior staff, volunteers from all across the board of the plant and Murph completed the new hiring guidelines. Cross-departmental groups like this had been working for some time now. It was Murphy's idea. These were his Impact Teams. His reasoning was that everyone in the plant had an impact every day they came to work. The impact could be good; it could be bad. Murphy was trying to get everyone to understand that they not only had a choice, but that they made a choice each day. This particular Impact Team was assigned to examine the plant's hiring process. The document they produced, although not complex, was designed to act as a guideline for future hiring decisions and for the overall process. It started with the simple premise Effie had first tossed at Murph: Listening was a more valuable skill than talking. It ended with the following primer on how hiring would be handled:

IMPACT HIRING

These 10 steps are designed to assist managers in the hiring process. The steps are not set in stone, but rather are guides that should be re-examined constantly so that we are always finding ways to improve our process, and thus improve our company, so that we may all benefit.

Tim Timmons

1. Make a newspaper happy – advertise

Where will the potential hires come from? From the company? From our community? From Indiana? From the Midwest? Nationally? Make a quality decision and advertise accordingly. Post jobs in the plant always. After that turn to the newspapers. Whether it's local or the state, newspapers tend to get the best results. This is the first and possibly the most important step in the hiring process. If you get no candidates, or if you don't get quality candidates, the rest of the process is pointless. Just like fishing, you don't fish for marlin with a bobber and a $4.99 Zebco reel on the White River. Look where the candidates are likely to be. Now that you know where to look, think long and hard about the bait you're using. If you make it so easy that anybody can get hired, don't be surprised two years later when you look at a staff that's under-performing. Put some hoops and rings out there for your candidates to jump through. If they can't get past that small of a hurdle, they're guaranteed to come to a full and complete stop the first time a dilemma at work strikes. Of course if your department never faces dilemmas . . . Ask those applying to do something: Write a letter explaining why they want to work here, or where they would like to be in five years (by the way, everyone asks that. Add a twist by asking them to explain what they're doing right now to make that a reality. If they answer that part of the question, you've got a winner!). Doesn't really matter what you ask, what you're trying to find out is if they can follow opening directions.

2. Gather Ye Rosebuds While Ye May

Carpe diem has its time and place, but this isn't it. Being bold is a great strategy, but at this point you should make Richard Nixon look like a wild-eyed liberal. Your most important mission at this point is not to make a hire. Let's repeat that all together. Your most important mission is not to make a hire. Your most important mission at this point is to eliminate candidates who won't be good for you or the company. Gather all your candidates and review their qualities. Did they jump through your hoops and rings? Do they possess the critical skills and qualities you need? While these might not be classified as absolute stop signs, count the following as yield or maybe information signs:

Job Jumpers: Those who go from job to job, or worse, industry to industry.

Gappers: Look for gaps of some time between jobs.

Slobs: Misspellings or sloppiness. If a coffee stain is present on their resume, what's that say about their work ethic or attention to detail? Also, how good is the quality of their copied resume or cover letter? Remember, this is the most important document they have. It is the key to their car payment, their mortgage, and their future. If it's sloppy or if it's just plain wrong, that speaks volumes.

On the other hand, here are some good things to look for:

Wow! Is their resume or paperwork creative and neat? Does it make you say wow?

A Mover and a Shaker: Does their job history indicate this is someone who moved up and got promotions? There's nothing wrong with being ambitious and leaving one job for a better one if it's done right. Do you have ambitious folks on your staff now? If you were promoted today, do you have someone in your department who's ready to step in and fill your job? If not, think about that when you hire.

A Good Packer: If there's a lot of information in a nice, small neat package, it shows they understand the importance of time and priorities. How they treat a potential employer now, is probably the best it will ever be. If they demand a lot of attention and time now, it will only get worse later if you hire them.

3. Do A Little Dance (with apologies to KC)

Now's the time to set up the dance. It starts with a telephone interview. Why? Because you're a busy person. Why bring in some of these folks who aren't likely to get an offer? It's a waste of your time and theirs. Set up a short phone interview with prepared questions (the same for all candidates). Your only goal at this stage is to whittle down the list to those you believe meet your needs and expectations.

Here are some things to cover:

1. What's Required: If they have to have a car or a valid driver's license, say so. If the job involves heavy lifting, say so. If there is a requirement such that they will not get the job unless they can meet that requirement, say so now. This could include salary, overtime expectations, travel, etc.

2. Screen, Screen and Screen Some More: Remember, your goal is to find out who won't make a good (whatever it is you're hiring). Ask questions to find that out. Be sure to stay within legal and ethical guidelines. There are certain things you can't, and shouldn't ask.

3. Promise Me No Promises: End without a commitment, unless you plan on sticking to it. It's tough, especially when you know there's no hope for the person on the other end, to end the call without trying to say something nice. But that won't do you or them any favors. False hope is just that, false. So, plan out the interview in advance. Script it. You can even script the small talk at the ending if that will help. "OK Mary, that's all the questions I have. I appreciate your time. Bye-bye." On the other hand if you slip and tell someone that you'll get back to them, follow up and do it.

4. Do Your Homework: Check for sub-references. Everyone knows what a reference on a resume will tell you, so why waste time calling them? Check instead with former places of employment (check with HR to get the reference release form). Let the candidate know you'll be checking. If they have a problem with that, you both can save a lot of time by stopping the process at that point. Let them know that before a final offer is made, you will need to talk with their current employer. Again, if they have a problem, find out now and save everyone some time.

4. Do The Math

OK, you've culled the list and you have only those left who you believe are still worth looking at. If you have an abundance of candidates, now's the time to set up another round of phone interviews. Before you do, however, here's a list of things you should do:

1. Wait a Minute, Mr. Postman: Mail them an application. We require applications on file. Now's the time to get that done if it's not done already.

2. Show Me The Money: If travel expenses are involved, be very clear on what will and will not be reimbursed. A rule of thumb: We'll pay expenses on key position interviews. We won't pay much for entry level. No blanket rules however. All these are on a case-by-case basis.

3. Where, When, How, Etc.: Let them know how to get here (mail, e-mail or fax a map), where to park, what door to come to, etc.

4. Establish a Schedule: Decide how long the interview will take and then add 15 minutes to half an hour. They may have some great questions, etc. If you schedule each one right on top of the other, you'll end up way behind schedule – and what does that tell the candidate about their future boss? Also, fires will inevitably crop up. Give yourself time between interviews to put them out.

5. Set the Table

Now your priorities are changing. Part of the interview is still designed to eliminate, but now you're starting to look at who you might want to eventually hire. Consequently, you should be putting your best foot forward as much as they should. If you were in their shoes, why would you want to work here? For the money? For the boss? For the surroundings? For the work? That's about all there is. So, polish things up (your current employees will appreciate that as well).
With this in mind, here are some tips to consider:

Prepare Your Questions Again: This time, not all your questions will be the same, although a fair amount will. If you don't ask the same questions, it's tough to compare. But you'll also want to ask some specifics based on their resume or application.

Show Them Attention: Put your phone on Do Not Disturb. Let your folks know that you'll be tied up for a specific time frame (and if you really want to score some points, let them know when you're done, too!). Do the little things that mean a lot. Does the person in for the interview want something to drink? Walk them back to the break room and give them a little tour. Talk to them in a friendly way about how the interview will work. Remember, they're nervous. Help alleviate some of that tension and you'll see a truer picture of who they are.

6. The Show

Now it's time for the nitty-gritty. Explain to your candidate that this is simply the process that we go through and that while you will ask the questions, they should feel free to take notes and ask their own questions. Give them a little background on the job and the company. Don't oversell. Get started then. Here are some tips and hints that might help:

COACHING SUCCESS

You Know Who You Are: Talk less and listen more. One study shows that the more an interviewer talks the more likely the interviewee is to be hired. Ask concise questions. Pulling teeth? If all you're getting is "yes" and "no," try to draw answers out with some of these: "Could you elaborate on that? Could you give me an example of what you mean? Help me understand what you meant by that? I'm not sure I understand; could you go on more? Could you help me with that answer?" Or, you can say nothing at all. Ten seconds of silence will draw out a lot of answers.

Take Notes and Notes and More Notes: Ever bought a car or a house after a lot of searching? After a while, it's tough to remember which one was which. Interviews are much the same. Take lots of notes so you'll remember each one.

Before It's Over, Did You: Did you learn what you wanted? You went into this with a goal? Did you accomplish it?

Before It's Over, Did They: Did they handle it well? If you threw them a hanging curveball, did they knock it out of the park or did they whiff? Were they enthusiastic? Did they burn their former or current employer (and their bridge to possible employment with our company)? Did they follow all instructions you gave? Did they dress appropriately? Did they ask questions, or sit silently?

Do They Fit: Looking at the candidate and knowing that chemistry is important, how do they fit with your team? How do they fit with you?

7. The Next Step

Where you go from here depends on a couple of things. Is the candidate an overnight guest or just an appointment? If it's overnight, plan out supper, etc. This brings with it a whole new set of responsibilities. If it's just for the duration of the interview, end it with whatever your plan is. At this point, you need to let them know that we will contact them (by mail, phone, e-mail) on where we go from here.

Again, Avoid Promises: If this isn't your top candidate (or even if it is at this point), don't tie yourself to a timetable. Circumstances change and you don't want them waiting on your Friday deadline the Wednesday after. Plan the ending.

Rank and File: Rank your candidates in the order you think they'll be most suited for the job. Bring in another opinion if you like. Look for reasons why it won't work, instead of why it will. It's much, much easier to avoid a problem at this point that it as after you've actually gone out and hired the problem.

More Interviews or Not: That's your next question. There's nothing wrong with second or even third interviews. If you feel it would help, do it. If not . . .

8. The Offer (they hopefully can't refuse)

When you've selected the person you want to make an offer to, get busy. Remember, this may not work out with the solution you are hoping for and you may have to drop back to candidate No. 2. So don't waste any time.

In Person Or Not: Ideally, when you make the offer, you'll want to be sitting across from each other. However, it's very possible that this won't happen. Decide on which and go.

Negotiating: Some parts of the offer can be negotiable, some can't. Decide on what you can work with and be ready to do so. For example, 401-K and such are out of your hands. Salary and hours are in your hands. Be ready. Have "yes" and "no" points already worked out. Don't decide on the spot. Emotions have no part in this process, and they will if you don't know your limitations (this also applies in the actual offer of the job. Never do that at the conclusion of an interview. Give yourself some time to get away and look back objectively.). On salary, no raise after 90 days. That's a game we don't play. Give them what we budget for the job up front and don't play games.

Don't Beat A Dead Horse: If it doesn't work out, move on. One rule of thumb though, if your top two candidates say no, start over. Unless you have an exceptionally deep talent pool, two's as deep as you want to go. If you're digging that deep into the pool, especially in an area of low unemployment, you are lowering your standards. Don't settle!

9. Set A Date

OK, you've gotten who you want, they want you and we're all set to begin a great relationship. Whoa, partner! Here are a few more tips for you to follow:

They Did Give Two Weeks, Didn't They: If, after all this, they don't give their current employer a proper (at least two weeks) notice, stop the show and bid them a nice life. If they end a relationship with that employer that way, you can count on them doing the same to you. We won't hire someone that way.

Give Them Details, Details, Details: OK, everything is great and we're all set. Get the start date and let them know where to park, what door to come in, where to hang their coat, etc. Be sure they know who to contact in case an emergency comes up. Help them prepare to be successful.

Don't Keep A Secret: Once the hire is made and the details are done, put out a memo to your staff and let the other department heads know.

10. Train, Train (take me to the promised land)

Wait, aren't we done yet? Nope. Now you're ready to

give your new hire all the tools to get off on the right foot.

Short staff, schmort staff: Chances are you've been without a full staff for at least a little while and survived. If you want to continue to work short-handed, throw your new hire into the mix and see how long they last. Set up a good training program and get them off on the right foot. The more training you do the first week or two, the less time you'll have to spend fixing problems later.

Be Smart on Training: Teach them what they need to know in order to do the job. A bunch of extra stuff that has nothing to do with nothing won't help. Enlist help on training. If you don't have to do it all yourself, don't. Make it a good process for everyone who is involved.

90 Days Isn't Very Far Away: When they're learning, make sure they know what's important – which is what they should be training on. Make sure they know what success looks like. Remember, the better they are, the easier your job is!

Murphy almost always liked the outcomes from the various Impact Teams. This one was no exception.

Chapter

<u>11</u>

When the accounting department dropped off the month-end report, Murph ripped open the large brown envelope the report came in. He flipped forward a couple of pages and ran his finger down to the bottom line, literally. He smiled, reached for the phone and hit the intercom button again.

"If I could have your attention please," he said, still feeling a little awkward talking to every one this way. "Several months ago I asked you to come to work and do your best every day. In other words, I asked you to come in and play to win. I just got the monthly report and I'm pleased to tell you that are now officially 7-2. That means entering the fourth quarter – historically our toughest – you have put yourselves into position to be successful. You are playing to win and it shows. I can't tell you all how proud I am to be on your team. Seven down, just three more to go!"

Murphy's announcement and the way he followed it up were the talk of the plant. After Murph got off the PA, he made the rounds in the plant, shaking hands, saying thanks to everyone he saw. As the shift ended, two long-time workers were walking toward their cars in the parking lot, rehashing the day's events.

"Did Coach come by your department?" the first one

asked.

"Sure did. Shook his hand, too."

"That guy could run for mayor if he wanted to. He just has a way, you know?"

"Yup, he could probably run for governor."

A third co-worker overheard the conversation.

"He's OK and all, but he's just a boss."

"He's more than that, sonny," the eldest of the trio chastised. "I've had plenty 'just a boss' before. This guy is a lot more than 'just a boss.'"

"Is that so? What makes him so much better?"

"I'll tell you what it is. He cares. He really does give a hoot and it shows. Sure, he wants to 'win,' as he calls it. But he wants all of us to win. And I'll tell you what; I've worked for a whole bunch of those who just want the glory all to themselves, and all the money that goes with it. That or they only want to catch you when something goes wrong, and then they're always looking for somebody to blame. You ask me, this Coach Murphy is my kind of boss. He looks for people who are winning, not losing."

MURPH'S PLAYBOOK

It's not a subtle difference. If a coach constantly criticizes a player, after a while the player tends to look toward the bench each time they make a mistake instead of concentrating on playing. In business, spending time with positive reinforcement yields much better results. Still not convinced? Look at school transfer rates where coaches constantly dwell on faults.

COACHING SUCCESS

Murphy was arranging a meeting with the Impact Team from Joseph's department so the group could give their recommendation on what to do with the department head vacancy. During his coaching career, there weren't many times when he was caught completely off guard, but he found himself in that unusual territory as the meeting opened.

"We've put together some metrics on how this might unfold," a young woman named Mandy began.

"Excuse me," Murphy interrupted. "Metrics?"

"Sure," she answered. "We thought it best to look at it from all angles."

"I agree," Murph said. "But what's 'metrics?'"

The silence that followed was awkward. Murphy noticed that everyone found something to look at other than him. Mandy looked like she would rather be somewhere else.

"Uh, you know, it's a way to put together facts," she said quietly.

Murphy was feeling a lot like the only one in the group who didn't get the punch line. It wasn't a feeling he was used to. He smiled. "You're going to have to help me here, Mandy. We didn't use a lot of metrics on the field."

Mandy took a deep breath and did what the guy in front of her had been teaching them for almost a year. Give your best effort and give it your all. Everything else will take care of itself. "Sure you did, Coach," she started. "You called it a game plan. This is just an analysis of numbers and facts broken down into a particular form. It's our way of playing 'what if.' Isn't that what you said you and your coaches did in coming up with a game plan for your next opponent?"

"You bet," he answered. "OK, I've got it now. Is metrics a term you guys use specifically in this department?"

This time the silence was really awkward. "No, Coach. It's a pretty common word in business."

It wasn't the first time Murph felt out of place. But it

was a feeling he definitely didn't like. However, he also knew that everyone else in the room felt a little funny, too. As a leader, they were his first responsibility. His bruised ego would heal.

"I knew I shouldn't have skipped those business 101 classes," Murph joked. "OK, what did your metrics show you?"

After the meeting ended and Murphy had gone out of the room, one of the group said, "I can't believe he didn't know. How do you run a company and not know that?"

"Because he understands what makes people tick and he does understand strategy," Mandy shot back. "Look, don't you think he could talk about . . . I don't know – pass options and run-blitzes and all kinds of terms we wouldn't know? Just because he doesn't know the latest business buzzword doesn't mean he doesn't know business."

"Run-blitzes? I don't know about run-blitzes," a guy named Mike said. "But metrics are pretty common."

"Yeah," Mandy said. "And so was EVA and CVA and paradigm and a thousand other terms we've heard along the way. I don't know that guys like Sam Walton and Walt Disney knew a whole lot about those terms either. Coach may not be up on the latest flavor of the month business fad or terminology, but if you don't think he understands business, take a look around. For Pete's sake, the guy has done more for this plant and the people who work here than any of his predecessors. And if I remember right, didn't that Trenz guy have a masters in some kind of applied manufacturing technology thing that none of us have ever heard of? And Mike, if I also remember right, you thought he was a pretty smart guy a little while ago when he came to us and said he wanted us to recommend where we go from here," Mandy said.

"OK, OK, I give," Mike said with his hands held up in surrender. "You've given me a new paradigm on this –

that is, if I'm still allowed to use that word."

It cracked everyone up.

Across the building, Murphy was just getting back to his office. "Effie, I need your help."

"Sure boss, what is it?"

"I need information on some business language . . ."

Hours turned into days and days into weeks. As the year wound down, the feeling was not unfamiliar to Murphy. It was something akin to a close football game. Clearly it didn't have the drama and the jump-out-of-your-seat-and-scream excitement that the game held. He didn't see how it really could be that way, though. A game was a set number of minutes on the clock and maybe three hours of an afternoon. This, this was life day in and day out. There were highs and lows certainly. But it wasn't the same. In some ways, Murphy thought, that was good. And in some ways it wasn't.

Murphy had always enjoyed watching his "boys" grow up during their four years with him. With few exceptions, each one came in a boy and left a man. Sure, there were a few who didn't make it for four years under Murph, but those were few and far between. People at the plant were as different as night and day. These were people with lives. They had children to care for. They had mortgages. It was real life, short and simple, long and complex. Back at U of I, it may have been his job, but it was still a game. Here, this was much more. It was a fact that Murphy never forgot in the entire year he had been there.

As for this particular "game," Murphy knew in his gut that they were going to win. The numbers that came in – now on a daily basis – looked good. Quotas were being surpassed routinely. The cost of doing business was at an all-time low because Murphy had given the front-line employees the ability to make changes, either through practice or recommendation. In short, the plant had never operated better. Part of the reason was the daily numbers. No one had ever asked the accounting department to come up with something like that before. But, Murphy reasoned, all the information was there. So, why couldn't a report be produced that gave the operating managers a strong tool to manage with? The only answer initially was because it hadn't been done before, but that didn't fly too far, and soon, everyone was looking at daily numbers and learning to be much more proactive.

Murphy also knew that something unforeseen could change everything. A fumble in a game could turn the tide (it would have to be a fumble and not an interception. That's because once in this position, only a stupid team put the ball in the air – and Murphy never, ever had a stupid team). In the plant, a mechanical breakdown could throw a literal wrench into the plans. Something could happen to a key client and the results would be deeply felt in the plant. Even a downturn in the local economy could make a difference. That was a part of the job Murphy absolutely hated. As a coach on the field, he felt there were very few things completely beyond his control. Yet in business, there were some very real factors that he couldn't do anything about. He likened it to a star player on the opposing team. Murphy couldn't control how much talent the other side had. It was his job to figure out a way to find a way to win regardless. Sometimes that meant doing everything possible to stop one

> **MURPH'S PLAYBOOK**
>
> *In this line of business, knowing where they stood each day was valuable. So, Murph found a way to give that tool to those who needed it and could benefit from it. Just because the tool had to be invented did not deter him. Don't let it deter you.*

COACHING SUCCESS

guy. By doing that, you made the other coach find a different way – hopefully one they weren't as good at – to beat you. For example, the Huskies played a team from West Virginia who had a receiver who would go on to play in the pros. The quarterback had a decent enough arm to get the ball to the receiver. But, the team had very few other weapons. So, Murphy double and even triple-teamed the receiver. He threw blitz after blitz at the quarterback. In doing so, he forced the opponent to run, something they weren't very good at.

Murphy smiled at the memory. Even with all the things they did, the outcome was in doubt until the very end. They did manage to shut down the wide receiver, but U of I's offense was also shut down for most of the day. The game was a scoreless deadlock until the fourth quarter. Then, with time winding down until just a few seconds were left, Murph's Huskies managed to kick about a 40-yard field goal that put them ahead, 3-0. Murph felt that was that, until he saw the star receiver trot onto the field from the other sideline to return the ensuing kick. The kid hadn't returned a kick all year, but the opposing coach was creative enough to recognize an opportunity and bold enough to take advantage of it. Murph wanted to bring his team back and make sure they knew how to handle the kick. However, he had used all his timeouts in getting the field goal, so he couldn't spend any extra time talking things over. He did manage to convey to the kicker to "squib" the ball, which is to kick it on the ground. He did, but as football bounces go, the ball traveled further than intended and it took one of those bounces, straight up into the future pro's hands. It marked the first time he had his hands on the football the entire game. Murph could, even after all these years, vividly recall how the kid broke one tackle and another as he brought the ball back up the field. Murph even remembered seeing the kid run full speed past him, graceful as can be, on the sideline. Just beyond the kid, Murph could still see that scoreboard clock it hit double zeros. One way or the other, the game was going to end on that play.

More than what happened next, Murph recalled how he felt standing on that sideline. On one hand, his hat was off to his opponent across the field. Faced with a tough situation, that coach had been innovative and Murph hadn't seen it coming. It was a lesson he still remembered. Perhaps he remembered because the sting of a loss never completely left a coach. Murph could still see the kid crossing the goal line, snatching victory from the proverbial jaws of defeat. It was the kind of moment that made sports special. With the outcome in the balance, a smart plan that was well executed made all the difference.

With about 10 weeks to go in the year, Murphy sat there and wondered if there wasn't something waiting to happen that he hadn't counted on.

Another one of Murphy's Impact Teams had just completed their work on a plant-wide recognition program and it was in Murphy's hands for the first time. Murph liked it. In essence, it took the service awards program and added performance.

The company had long recognized those employees who celebrated anniversaries. At the completion of five years, a pin was given. Each five years thereafter, a nice piece of jewelry marked the event.

Murph didn't have a problem with recognizing those who demonstrated staying ability. But he did think that it was a problem when it was the only recognition. He guessed it came from his coaching background. No matter how much everyone liked, or for that matter, didn't like coaches. They stayed or went based almost entirely on their performance. If a coach was a consistent winner, he had a job as long as he wanted. If the winning stopped, so did the employment usually. It was just another one of those things that puzzled Murphy when he came into the business world. The reward system at the plant was based on longevity, not on results. Merit raises were talked about, but in the end, everyone got a raise on their anniversary each year. It was one of the first things Murphy changed when he came on board.

"Why should someone get a raise just because the calendar turns?" Murphy asked during a meeting with some of the senior staff.

"Because they deserve it," Charles had fired back.

"Help me understand that," Murph had said.

"What is there to understand? They complete another year. The cost of living goes up. They get a raise. It's the way we've always done it."

Thinking back on it now still puzzled the coach turned CEO. For the life of him, he couldn't see how people were "entitled" to raises. For that matter, that sort of thinking led to the feeling of being "entitled" to the job. Murph changed all that when he told everyone that raises would be based on merit. If people performed well and achieved things, why should they have to wait a year for a raise? If someone did something that was significant and created a "win" for the company, it only made sense to reward them and reward them quickly.

The move hadn't gone over without conflict, nor had Murphy expected it to. But it was the right thing to do and the sooner it was done the sooner things would improve. Almost a year later, the effects were proving him right.

"So, how many different awards have you created?" Murphy asked Marti. She had been the obvious choice to head the task Murph had

> **MURPH'S PLAYBOOK**
>
> Sports teams rarely have an "entitlement" culture, yet businesses sometimes do. How much does it hold back a company? A lot.

thought. Marti was always thought of as one of the nicest members of the senior staff. She was clearly well liked. Murph thought that this job might help her improve some of her leadership skills and add some respect.

"We've decided that each department will have their own monthly awards," Marti began. "Some of those will be selected by the department team members, while others will be selected by the department management. It's all broken down and explained in this document," she said handing Murphy a three-ring binder. "And with that, I'd like to ask Linda to explain the next part."

Murph frowned to himself. This was an opportunity for Marti to step up and take the lead, and here she was sitting down. He decided to talk to her afterward, in private.

Linda explained that the next tier of recognition would be division awards. The senior division head would select these. The criteria for winning such an award was in the binder Murphy had, Linda explained. Then she handed off to the third member of the small committee, Gary.

He explained that the last set of monthly awards were plant-wide honors and the senior staff, with Murph's involvement, would choose these as well.

Gary and Linda then said before they handed the presentation back to Marti, they wanted to explain to Murphy how much they appreciated how Marti had handled this process. She and they had met and discussed each step. However, Marti had given them the freedom to do things their way – within the guidelines she had established. They felt very empowered in the process and had truly enjoyed and appreciated the opportunity Marti had given them.

Murph smiled a big smile. Check that meeting afterward, he thought to himself, proud of Marti for stepping up to the plate.

COACHING SUCCESS

He looked to Marti to continue and noticed that she was blushing. "The last set of awards we've agreed on are annual awards. The first one is for attendance. We think if anyone shows up every day without exception, they should be honored."

> **MURPH'S PLAYBOOK**
>
> *Good coaches don't jump to conclusions. They wait until they have all the facts. Doing so in this case as a matter of routine saved Murphy from an embarrassing mistake.*

"Wait a minute," Murph interrupted. "We've struggled a lot trying to teach people that it's about performance, not attendance."

"We agree," Marti said. "But the first requirement in performing is showing up. We also have not attached any monetary value to this award. It's a plaque.

"The second honor is what we decided to call the 'Playing to Win' award. It will be for as many people who qualify. All the breakdowns are in the binder, but in short it means that someone has to do something measurable that significantly impacts the business."

"Did you define 'significant,'" Murphy asked.

"In general broad brush strokes only," Marti answered. "We felt that the important part is to ensure that it's measurable and it's a big deal. However, what might be a big deal in one area, or even in one year, might be different to another area or another year. We were comfortable with the process being decided at the highest levels of this plant's management."

"One concern we had was that this would turn into a 'pass-around' award," Linda added. "We've included some language that specifically points out that this could go to the same department, or even the same person, more than once."

"That's right," Gary tossed in. "We tried very hard to point out that performance is the absolute decider. It's not a popularity contest or an attempt to share the glory. We think," he said looking at the others and smiling a little, "that the culture of this company now understands that."

"And our last award is what we called the MVP, Most Valuable Performer," Marti said. "We just thought it made a lot of sense. You've got all of us thinking in terms of winning and that sort of thing. When you think like that, these names just made sense. The MVP is the one person in the plant who had the most measurable positive impact. Again, all the details are in there."

Murph flipped through the pages. Some of the awards had money attached, some had time off, and some had trophies or plaques or jewelry. Overall, he liked what he saw, with just one small question. "Is there anything else?" he asked.

"Just eligibility," Marti said. "We think someone should have to be part of the team for at least a year before they're eligible to win anything." Murph liked that. On his teams, freshmen had to earn some respect through their performance as well as logging some time. This made sense. "Besides that, there's only one group who we don't think should be included in these awards, the senior staff."

And that brought a huge smile to Murphy. He always thought that coaches, and now he and his senior staff, were rewarded enough through pay, perks, etc. Recognition or publicity should go to others. Marti was indeed growing. Murphy decided to go ahead and meet with her afterward. He wanted to be sure to tell her how proud he was of her and what a great job she had done in this leadership role.

The training programs that Murphy had begun throughout the plant had taken on a life of their own.

COACHING SUCCESS

Once a month most departments held fun and spirited competitions. Bea's expanded department was doing just that today. As usual, Bea was the loudest cheerleader. "C'mon, you can do it, just a little more," she encouraged one of her staffers as their fingers furiously flew over the keyboard. The record of 132 words in a minute had stood for three months and was in danger of falling. The crew looked on in anticipation.

When the bell (actually a digital egg timer) dinged, the clacking stopped. All eyes turned to the top right hand corner of the monitor where the number 137 flashed. A cheer went up.

"I used to swim when I was little," Bea said loudly to the group. "I had a coach who used to tell us all the time, 'you never make state cuts at the meet; you make state cuts in practice.' Well, let me tell you, this practice has paid off in a new department record! Pizza for everybody!"

Murph walked in at that minute to hear the cheers. "Did I miss it?" he asked. "Did you get it?"

"Did we get it?" Bea mocked. "Did we get it? Why coach, look at Barb over there. Was there any real doubt?"

Murph shook Barb's hand and asked what the new standard was.

"It's 137, Coach," she answered.

"Congratulations, Barb," he said. "That's just outstanding."

"Never could've done it without my boss," Barb said pointing to Bea. "She's the best coach there is . . . " Barb stopped and remembered who she was talking to. "Present company excluded, of course, sir."

Everyone joined Murphy in the biggest belly laugh he had had for quite a while. "That's quite alright, Barb," he said. "I think I agree with your first statement."

Denise's department was enjoying another phenomenal year. Though how much of the results were because of Denise and how much her staff really accounted for was a question in Denise's mind. Denise was sure of one thing, if it hadn't been for her, the numbers would've been a lot different. Certainly the people who worked for her had provided value and what had been accomplished wouldn't have happened without them. But then again, it wouldn't have happened without her either. That much she knew and that much she was dead certain of.

Although she had learned a lot from this football coach, she still wasn't sure that at the end of the day he was the right guy to lead the plant. Certainly he had been a perfect transition from the previous flops Smith had brought in. He injected life where none had been. He brought hope and optimism. That's what coaches did, though, wasn't it? So, other than cheerleading, what did he really do? When it came to abilities, what did he bring to the table? Denise still thought she was light years ahead of anywhere the famous T.J. Murphy might be.

On the other hand, Oscar Torres and Dave Eads felt they had benefited greatly from Murphy's leadership. Both guys had been sports fans and that had helped them quickly buy into Murphy's plan. They had also grown as leaders as they watched Murphy generously pass around the credit; watched him meticulously plan for the unexpected; watched him pay great and close attention to detail; watched him make those around him better. And although neither one of the pair would admit it now, they had their doubts when Walt Smith's crazy idea had been announced that day nearly a year ago.

Oscar had even started a diet, something that pleased his wife to no end. He had been in Murphy's office one afternoon. Murphy had asked him what he wanted to do after his working life had ended. Oscar talked about doing some traveling, about seeing his grandchildren, things like that. Murphy looked him straight in the eye and said it was too bad Oscar would never get to do any of that. What did he mean, Oscar had asked a little indignantly? Well, Murphy had started, as a former football coach he did know a thing or two about physical fitness. Knowing that, there was no doubt in his mind that Oscar wasn't going to live very long after retirement, that is if he made it that far.

Oscar remembered being at first shocked and angry. Who did Murphy think he was telling him that? Murphy had leaned forward and put his hand on Oscar's arm. "I'm just an old coach, Oscar," he had said. "And I may not know much, but I do know if you don't make some life changes, you're not going to be around to enjoy all those things you talked about." Murphy was looking Oscar straight in the eyes, not blinking one bit.

Oscar looked down. He had always been heavy; it was just a way of life. He didn't even know what he could do about it. Not to worry, Murphy had said. The trainer over at the college was a close friend and Murphy was sure he'd work with Oscar, if Oscar wanted. Should Murphy put in a call? Oscar thought for about three seconds and said yes.

Dave Eads had benefited from a similar visit with Murphy one day. They were talking about the numbers in Dave's department, which weren't up to par. Dave was telling Murphy how much he enjoyed working for him and how much he was learning. Murphy leaned over at one point and looked Dave square in the eye.

"Dave, cut the crap. Your numbers suck and either you have to get them up or we're going to have to figure out something else."

The statement had caught Dave completely by surprise. He immediately started back-pedaling, trying to explain why the numbers were below expectations. Murphy never even let him get to first base.

"Dave," Murphy had started. "Why do you spend so much time worrying about what I think? Why don't you worry instead about what your people think? Spend more time figuring out how you can make your numbers rather than how you can explain missing them. Dave, you're a great guy and I want you on this team. You've got 20 years with this company. But something's got to give in your area or else I've got to start figuring out why. You don't want that, and trust me when I tell you, I don't want that either."

For maybe the first time in his professional life, Dave looked at his boss and said, "I honestly don't know how to do it. I've tried, but I just don't know how."

Murphy looked at Dave for a long time and asked. "Do you want to?"

"Yes," Eads said quietly. "I honestly do, I just am not sure I can."

"Then what we do is get you the tools you need to do the job, Dave," Murph said. "There's a couple of things coming up we can get you involved with that will help you. I promise you I'll work as long and as hard as you do for this. Together, we can make it work."

Dave was stunned. Never before had he been this honest with a boss. The reaction was certainly not what he expected.

Murphy had once again gained a loyal employee.

It hadn't worked with Billy Polaski. Billy knew without a doubt that the plant revolved around he and his department. He knew that if he went somewhere else, the plant would likely fall apart. Never mind that he felt the same way about the company he left before coming here and it was doing just fine in his absence. The problem with Billy was that his talent was only surpassed by his ego. On the other hand, he was smart enough to at least know when to tone it down. When Murphy was getting irritated with him, he would turn the volume down a notch or two until things blew over. Billy knew that Murphy had enough other things to worry about that he wouldn't spend too much time looking in Billy's area, especially since his numbers were so good.

What Billy didn't know and didn't understand was that Murphy was smarter than Billy gave him credit for. Murphy knew what kind of talent he had in Billy, but he also knew that Billy was a ticking time bomb waiting to go off. Murphy could see Billy easily becoming the next Charles. He had tried talking to Billy a couple of times to no avail. He told Billy that as talented as he was, winning never came at all costs. He tried to get across the message that, as important as the numbers were, the way business was done was even more important. The way employees were treated was more important. The way you presented information to customers was more important. It was a message that fell on deaf ears. After all, when you already knew everything, what would be the need to listen?

Not all the members of the senior staff had stepped up to the plate, Murphy thought sitting alone in his den. There was a fire in the fireplace and the winter wind sounded cold and uninviting outside. The plant was in the last weeks of the year. The team had a record of 9-2. Murphy was pretty certain that the challenge he had issued what seemed like a lifetime ago was going to be met. The plant had played to win, and win it was going to do. Murphy had to admit that Billy and Denise were two of several reasons they were going to win. Still, he was disappointed with both of them. Even after all this time, they put themselves first and they still had egos that required constant attention. When Effie had put together a virtual dictionary of business terms for Murph a while back, she had included the term "high maintenance." Since no one but Murph would ever see it, Effie had pasted pictures of Denise and Billy beside the phrase. Still, part of the definition was that only those with lots of talent could be termed high maintenance. Effie's explanation was that if someone who fit that description wasn't really, really good, they wouldn't be worth the trouble to keep around.

That was another difference between this and coaching. Coaches who made sure it was more about them than it was about the kids or the school weren't real popular with their peers. They might end up with jobs, but they didn't have many friends. There was an old story about those coaches. In the past year, Murphy found out that it was an old business story, too. In football, it was always about a new, slick coach taking over a program from a long-time veteran. Before leaving the office for the last time, the old coach who knew and used all the tricks of the trade takes the new coach aside. He asks the upstart if he has a plan for what he's going to do when he loses some games he shouldn't. The new cocky coach who can't imagine losing many games says things like practice harder, spend more time on film, etc. The grizzled old veteran shakes his head and tells the youngster that he's left him three envelopes, clearly marked one, two and three. When the going got really tough, open the first one, and so on.

So the veteran coach takes his leave and the young coach settles in. His first year he wins a couple of games and loses a couple. However, about mid-season his team takes a nosedive and it gets ugly. Fans are irate, the media is on his back and even the players are grumbling. Remembering the envelopes, he gets into the desk and opens the envelope marked No. 1.

"Blame the old coach," it reads.

So, he lays the current string of problems on the old coach and everyone simmers down. The team starts winning again and life is good. Things go along OK until another down period hits. Same thing. Fans and media up in arms. It's ugly again. He opens the second envelope.

"Blame the players."

He does and everything quiets down again.

Some time later, more rough times. Again, he goes to

the desk and opens the final envelope. Inside it says, "Prepare three envelopes."

Murphy loved telling the story to his new coaches. He always told it in terms of something that happened to him at an earlier job. They always took it in – hook, line and sinker – until the very end when they realized they'd been had. Murph always got a great laugh, while at the same time making a point about not blaming others.

> **MURPH'S PLAYBOOK**
>
> *'Nuff said? No one respects the person who never takes responsibility. Sure, they might be happy to take the credit when things go good. But as soon as the pendulum swings, as it inevitably does sometimes, they are quick to point the finger of blame elsewhere. Think of people you know who shoulder the responsibility, even when it's not their fault. Behind the scenes, they'll work it out. But in front of everyone else, they're quick to stand up and catch the heat. Former President Harry Truman said the buck stops here. Great coaches and leaders know that philosophy well.*

Murph reflected back on the year at hand. He had been doing this annually sometime during the week of the last game for years. Usually, the weather was about like it was tonight, crisp and cold. The fire felt good though and Murph always felt it was a good practice to look back.

He had started the year not knowing what he was getting into. He had a senior staff that consisted of eight people. Two of those were gone, although Murph knew one was unnecessarily tragic. Then again, both were unnecessary, Murph thought. Every opportunity to turn around and stay was given to Charles. The final decision was more Charles' than anyone else's, Murph knew. So it might have been something unnecessary that became necessary. That was another difference between coaching and business. Sometimes things were more complicated than they needed to be.

The heat from the fire caused Murphy to roll the stool his feet were propped on away from the fireplace. Julie often warned him that he was going to catch that stool on fire as close as he got to the fireplace. But he always figured when his feet got hot, he'd move it and that would be that – simple, not complicated.

He looked around the room. The big oak cabinets that covered one wall were full of shadows. The only light in the room came from the fire that was dying down just a bit. Murph got up and put two new logs on top, adjusting them to just the right position with the blackened poker. The crackles and pops sounded reassuring as he fell back into the over-stuffed leather chair.

Murph knew he had been good for the plant. On the other hand, some of it hadn't been that hard. He had never been afraid to fail in his entire life. It came with the self-confidence that Murphy thought more people should have. Had he failed at this, or anything else, Murphy always knew he would pick up the pieces and move on. He supposed coaching had taught him that as well. No matter how good you were, some games were going to be lost. It was never the end of the world, just a disappointment, a lesson to be learned and to move on from. He had taught that to at least some of the folks who worked for him. It was always disappointing when he knew there were those who didn't learn some of the lessons he tried to impart. But every team, every year, had some. This would be no exception.

Ironically, another lesson that Murphy always tried to pass along was learned not from football or business.

COACHING SUCCESS

He learned it when his wife dragged him to an opera years ago. Julie had gotten tickets to an upcoming opera – that was the problem for a guy like Murphy who worked at a college, there were way too many events that Julie called a taste of culture. Murphy dreaded going and had actually tried to get out of it several times. Julie was having none of that though and Murphy was smart enough to know when it was time to give in. So he had rented a tux and gone. Amazingly, he learned three things that he shared with his football teams, and now with his business colleagues.

First, opera takes a great deal of practice, like anything that's worth anything in life. The movements were perfectly in sync. The orchestra performed flawlessly. As Murph watched, he did what he always did. He translated everything into football coaching. The preparation and the practices or rehearsals must have been a huge challenge.

Second, opera takes trust. There were several times where the female "fell" backward into someone's arms. It reminded him of the French circus troupe he had seen perform some amazing stunts. In the end, the person in mid-air had to trust their buddies.

And lastly, the singing left Murphy wondering why he had dreaded coming. It was so good and so . . . powerful that he went out and bought the recording so he could listen to it in his office.

"What makes it *that* good?" asked one of his coaches.

"You have to see it, to experience it," Murph explained. "They don't hold anything back. They just go all out. There's no middle ground. They can't sing tentatively. It's all or nothing." The same was true with that circus, Murph thought. It was also true on a football field. Although the bold weren't always rewarded, those who were tentative almost never were. You had to give it everything you've got if you want to be successful. Again, Murph knew that more people in the plant understood that lesson now than did when he walked in the door.

That reminded him of a conversation he and Joseph had just a week or so before the accident. Joseph had been saying that while he couldn't argue with the success the plant was enjoying, he wanted to caution Murphy to slow down a little. Murphy was trying to point out that passiveness wasn't a strategy he agreed with. They had talked for the better part of an hour, neither agreeing with the other. Looking back, Murph wished the conversation had gone differently.

> **MURPH'S PLAYBOOK**
>
> *Tentativeness is one of the biggest limiting factors in sports, in business, in life. This is not to suggest moving forward without planning or forethought. Just that what Murphy thought is certainly true: "Although the bold weren't always rewarded, those who were tentative almost never were."*

That was another difference between football and business. In football, there weren't lots of different agendas. Sure, the coaches might disagree when putting in the game plan. One coach might see the opponent as weak against the pass and push for more passing plays. Another coach would argue that their strength was the run and they shouldn't abandon their bread and butter. In the end though, the game plan would be hammered out and all the coaches would be on the same page.

In business, no matter how much success they had, Murph knew that a couple of his team members just weren't going to get on board. In coaching, that would have been unacceptable. In business, it was inevitable. Murphy decided that business teams needed those who shared the vision, the goal of what a win was. They did not necessarily have to agree on how to get there. The hierarchy was so different from the coaching world. In football, if the coach was the target of fans called "boo-birds," those boos came from the outside. In business, the leader was often the target of those same boo-birds – but they were from the inside. At the plant, that was very clearly the case when Murphy started. Although it wasn't nearly as true now, it wasn't and wouldn't ever be completely erased.

In the end, that was an adjustment that Murphy made. It wasn't one he necessarily liked. But he had never confused the plant with the football field. There were similarities. There were differences. This was one of the differences.

Murphy looked at the clock and realized he had been sitting there for hours. The fire had dwindled to a glow and he realized he was cold. He got up, closed the glass doors on the fireplace and headed up to bed.

The next morning, Murph's mind wandered on the drive to work. He hadn't slept well the night before. When he arrived at the plant, Murph made sure to smile and say "G'morning" to everyone he passed – something he thought very important to always do. But it took some effort this morning.

When Effie brought him a cup of coffee and tried to make some small talk, she could tell something was bothering her boss. Although she hadn't seen it very often, she had seen him this way a few times – the biggest being the whole debacle with Charles. Whatever it was, she hoped it wasn't that serious – and she hoped it wouldn't last long. Murphy was the best boss she ever had and she liked keeping him happy.

The phone startled her out of her concern. "Mr. Murphy's office."

"Is Coach, uh, Mr. Murphy in?" a man's voice on the other end asked.

"Let me check," she said, knowing full well that he was sitting at his desk. It was an old habit from a previous boss who used to duck lots of calls. "May I ask who's calling?"

"Sure," the man said – and didn't say anything else.

Effie waited a minute. She didn't get flustered very often, but that answer caught her off guard. "Uh, who may I say is calling?"

"Talbot," the voice laughed. "Nick Talbot. You didn't ask who I was, you asked if you could ask."

"Cute," Effie thought, seriously considering accidentally disconnecting the call. Instead, in her best professional voice she told the practical joker to please hold.

"Coach," Effie said over the intercom. "There's some smart . . . guy on the phone named Nick Talbot who . . ."

Before Effie could finish, Murph had already grabbed the phone.

"Nick! How the heck are you?" Murph asked his long-time friend and former coaching rival.

"A lot better without you on the sideline," Talbot laughed. "It feels pretty good to have the Sledgehammer for a change!"

Murph only winced a little. While he hated that his beloved Huskies had lost the annual slugfest this year, he was truly happy for his old friend.

"I understand, Nick," he said. "So, how's the family?"

"Doing great. Listen, what are you doing Tuesday?"

"Working, why? What's up?"

"The annual coaches golf outing," Talbot said. "I could never get you to play when you were coaching. But I figured now that you're a big, hot-shot business executive, you've probably played a bunch."

"Still haven't," Murph said. "I will say there're lots of chances to play, but I haven't picked up the game yet."

"Well, it's high time," Talbot said. "Besides, there's something I want to talk to you about and I figure a good time would be riding around in a golf cart with a cold beer or two."

Murph only thought for a second. What the heck?

Just being on this end of the conversation was the best he had felt in a week. "Sure, Nick. I'd love to. Want to share what it is you want to talk about?"

"See you Tuesday," was all Talbot said before hanging up with a laugh.

Monday night, Murphy dug into the depths of the basement and found his golf clubs and shoes. When he brought them upstairs, Julie smiled. Her husband had a spring in his step she hadn't seen in a little while.

Murph was pulling his clubs out of the back of the Jeep when Talbot put him in a bear hug from behind.

"Murph, you son of a gun, you look great. How ya been?"

"Hey Nick," he said. "You sure about this? I don't even remember the last time I actually played outside of a miniature golf course."

Talbot took one look at Murph's clubs and shoes and burst out laughing.

"You going to play with those or sell them for antiques?" Talbot chuckled. "I haven't seen real wood heads outside an antique store for at least 20 years. Let me see the bottom of your shoes . . . That's what I thought. C'mon, Coach. Let's get to the pro shop and get those metal spikes changed. Maybe we can rent some clubs, too . . ."

Murph had always been a pretty good athlete himself, and with a little coaching, got a little better each hole. It was a lot easier playing in a scramble, or captain's choice. Murph learned that the format had each one of the four players hitting off the tee. They then went to the best of the four shots and everyone played from that spot. Murph wasn't the least bit disappointed that none of his tee shots were used. But he was getting frustrated that very few of his shots went where he intended. On the other hand, he was more than pleased to share some time with a friend he hadn't seen for a while.

"So, what's the big surprise," Murph asked. "Did the Bears call with your dream job?"

"Nah, actually, I'm not going to wait on the Bears any longer," Talbot said. "And, you understand, this will be their loss. I'm moving on."

"Where to?" Murph asked, surprised. He always thought his friend would retire from his current school.

"It's not 'where to,' it's 'what to.'"

"Huh?"

"I'm following my hero T.J. Murphy and I'm retiring," Talbot said.

"Wow," Murph said. "I sure didn't expect that. Well, congratulations, Nick. What brought all this about?"

"Oh, just this and that. The wife and I have a cabin up in the woods and we're spending more and more weekends up there. We're finding it harder to come back on Sunday nights. So, we just decided to make the move a permanent one."

"Well, good for you," Murph said. "I sure appreciate you taking the time to tell me, too. I think you'll enjoy it."

"How the heck would you know?" Talbot laughed. "Looking at those bags under your eyes, I'm guessing you're working harder now than when you were coaching."

"No, not harder. Well, sort of," Murph said. "It's hard to explain. The hours are actually a lot better. No all-nighters breaking down film, that sort of thing. On the other hand, there's no off-season either. But it is a different kind of work and it does wear on you."

"I can tell, Murph. When are you going to really retire? You and Julie are more than welcome to spend some time up in the woods with us. Great fishing up there. And there's a pretty little 18-hole course that hardly anybody knows about. The owner there is an alum and we can play anytime."

"Thanks, Nick. Julie and I will take you up on it sometime."

The two friends pulled their cart up to the next shot.

COACHING SUCCESS

They were in the middle of the fairway, thanks to Talbot's drive, and about 150 yards out. All his playing partners were certainly polite, because they always let Murphy hit first. He pulled out his Sam Snead 5-iron and addressed the ball. He started the swing slowly, making contact with the intent of landing the little white ball near the flag. Instead, he grunted as it headed off into the trees on the right.

"Sheesh, Coach," Talbot laughed. "I'm sure glad you could coach better than you play golf, otherwise you and Julie might have starved. On the other hand, you guys did have to eat that cafeteria food!"

"Yeah, yeah," Murph muttered. "Everybody's a comedian."

That night at supper, Murph told Julie all about Nick Talbot's decision to retire. He told her about the open invitation they had to the cabin. He did not spend much time telling her about the golf game.

"You almost sound a little envious, dear," she said, prodding her husband just a tiny bit.

"Envious?" Murph asked. "No, not envious. Well, no. I mean, I don't think so."

Julie just looked at him. "OK."

"No, I mean what's to envy? I already retired from coaching. This is different."

"OK."

"OK what?"

"Nothing, dear."

"C'mon Jules, what?"

"It just seems like you've been a little less happy lately," she said. "And then Nick calls and you're like a kid at Christmas. You've been looking forward to today for almost a week."

Murph thought about it. He was too smart to just discount what his wife was saying. She knew him too well. The truth was that he had been thinking a lot lately about his original decision to retire.

"What do you think?" he asked.

"I think you look tired," she said. "Are you still happy working every day?"

"Overall, yes," he answered. "But it's not what it was. Business is different than coaching. I do know that I'm glad I coached all those years and then went into business rather than the other way around. I just don't know if I'm cut out to do this for 20 or 30 years."

"Well, you don't have to be," she said. "When you and Walt Smith agreed to this, neither of you set a timetable."

"I know," Murph said. "The thing is, he asked me to do a job, and I think we've done it. If I would decide to retire, he'd have to be happy with what we've accomplished."

"I know that, dear," she said. "Are you telling *me* that, or trying to convince yourself?" Julie knew her husband better than she knew anyone in the whole world. She was pretty sure he was working around to a decision. She also knew that he had to be completely satisfied that it was the right thing to do, or else he'd never do it.

"You know me," he said. "I agreed to do something and I won't balk at that. But in a lot of ways, that plant is ready to take the next step, and having someone with more working, technical knowledge than me makes some sense."

Murphy continued talking his way through it. Julie just listened. She knew that her husband wasn't just "justifying" a decision he either wanted or had already reached. That wasn't T.J. Murphy's way. She had sat through this process many times before. Murphy would list all the different facts and factors as best he knew. He would ask her opinion. He would listen. He might even gently argue, or expect her to. In the end, she knew it was a process that had served him well in making big decisions for a long time. She didn't expect this to be any exception.

Chapter 12

Bea knocked on Murph's open door and came in without waiting for a response. It had taken a while for Murphy to get her to stop waiting for permission.

"G'morning, Coach, got a minute?" she said cheerfully.

"Always," Murph smiled back. "What's up?"

"Well, I need to order some more thank you cards," she said. Murphy's wife had actually come up with the idea of having thank you cards designed and printed for the plant. Each one had pre-cut slots for those dollar coins and told the recipient that it was just a small thank you for a job well done. They were cheap, but effective. People loved getting them. One by-product was that it increased sales of coffee and cold drinks in the break area, and increased idea sharing and camaraderie.

"Uh, well, Effie always orders those," Murph said, a little confused. Bea knew that as well.

"OK," she said, adding – a little mischievously – "or I could just get some from Billy or Denise. I don't think they've used very many of theirs."

"Now Bea," Murph started, but couldn't continue. Bea was the one and only member of the senior staff who Murph confided in more and more as time went on. He wasn't going to tell her to play nice when he knew she was right.

"So what's on your mind, Bea?" he asked. "I don't think you wanted to come in here just to let me know you ran out of something."

"The numbers will be in tomorrow," she said.

"Yup."

"We're going to do it, we're going to finish 10-2," she said.

"Yup."

"So, what are we going to do about it? Mum's the word from Effie, and," she said, raising her voice, "everyone knows that Effie is never quiet about anything."

"Bait me all you want, you're not getting anything out of me," came the reply from the outer office.

Murph and Effie had actually planned quite an event. When everyone came to work in the morning, they would see notices posted that there would be a mandatory plant meeting at 3 that afternoon. Once there, Murph would make the announcement accompanied by balloons, confetti and a ragtime band. After years of coaching, Murph knew about locker room celebrations. This one would be a good one.

"Guess you'll need to show up at work tomorrow and see what happens," Murph smiled. "I guess I haven't thought too much about it."

"Posh!" Bea tossed back. "You think about everything."

"So, is that what you're doing, trying to figure out tomorrow?"

"Not exactly," she said. "I want to ask you a question – that is, if you don't mind. It's sort of personal."

"Not at all," Murph said. "You know you can ask anything."

"What happens after tomorrow?"

"What do you mean?"

"I think you know."

Murphy took a deep breath. "How much time have you got?"

The next day everyone saw the signs when they came

to work. It may well have been the worst surprise party in history. Everyone knew they had made it. The only question in their minds was how it would be handled. With Murphy's history, they were eager in their anticipation.

When the afternoon rolled around, Murphy called the senior staff to his office 15 minutes before the plant meeting. As they walked in, Murph handed each one an envelope.

"It's just a little something to say thank you from Walt and I," Murph explained. "This is over and above your bonus plans. You guys have done a phenomenal job and we just wanted to find an extra way to say thank you. Everyone in the plant will also be getting a bonus today."

"Coach, I think I can speak for all of us when I say thank you so much," Dave said. "You've made such a difference for all of us, and for me. Whatever is in this envelope wouldn't have happened without you."

"Dave, Bea, Marti, Oscar, Denise and Billy, I can't tell you what this year has meant to me," Murph said. "We achieved a goal that is pretty amazing. The neat part is we never would've achieved it without all of us and our teams working together. Ladies and gentlemen, thank you all. I want you to understand that I've had the honor of being involved in some pretty special teams in my lifetime. This will be one of the best."

The meeting was at the old movie theatre across the street. Effie had arranged to have it rented for the afternoon. She had also arranged for a cleaning crew afterward.

Everyone from the plant was there. Literally. Amazingly, attendance was 100 percent. On cue, the curtain began to open and confetti and balloons were released from the ceiling. Spotlights came on and began a wild rotation over the entire inside of the theater.

Backstage, Murph watched the celebration with a smile on his face. He certainly did not get into this job for the personal satisfaction and glory. But watching the people from the plant bat around balloons and shake confetti from their hair was giving him a pretty good feeling. Still, it was different from football.

On cue from Effie, he walked through the curtain to applause that built until it resulted in a standing ovation. Walt Smith also was present, to Murphy's surprise, and was standing in the front row applauding wildly. Murph squinted and looked around. Most of the senior staff were smiling the biggest smiles he had seen since he walked in the door. More importantly, everyone was smiling.

It hit Murphy that they had won. Not just won the year, the 10-month challenge he had given everyone what seemed a lifetime ago. They had won by making this celebration belong to everyone there. It wasn't just a celebration for Walt Smith. It wasn't just for Murphy. It wasn't just for the senior staff. The celebration was for Effie, for Linda, for Gary, for Cheryl, the list went on. The celebration was for and about everyone. It was just like his football teams of day's past. Individual achievement always helped, but no running back ever won a football game by themselves. No quarterback. No receiver. No linebacker. No defensive end. No guard. No tackle. No matter how good anyone was, they didn't – and couldn't – win a game alone. It always took a team effort.

That's exactly what had happened here. There were some great individual efforts during this year. Bea was the first one who came to mind. But how could Murph forget Marti and the growth she had gone through. Oscar and Dave had each made giant leaps. Even Denise and Billy turned in huge numbers that contributed significantly to the bottom line.

So Murph walked up to the podium, smiled and waved. Even with that, it took a full two minutes before the applause began to die down.

"Wow," Murphy started. "I haven't had that kind of response since I told the football team that practice had been called off for a week because the school had a flu epidemic. Look, you all know why we're here. So let me

COACHING SUCCESS

be the first to congratulate each of you. You pulled off the impossible and you've just completed a perfect 10 straight months of hitting budget!"

The cheer that went up this time was much louder than the first one. Murph could do little more than stand there and wait until it subsided a little bit. He waited. And waited a little more. Unbelievably to even himself, Murphy was actually feeling a little embarrassed by all this.

Finally, after what seemed like an awfully long time, the applause began to die down. "Wow," Murph said a little ruffled. "I want to share some thoughts with you about this year and what you've achieved.

"As you all know, I've been a football coach all my life. I've watched kids win and lose football games. You know, during that time, I couldn't imagine anything more important. Now, I look around at all of you and I know what's truly important in life.

"I want to take this opportunity to say thank you to each and every one of you. While I appreciate the credit that many of you have thrown my way, the credit, as Theodore Roosevelt used to say, belongs to you who have been in the arena. You are the ones who have gotten dirty. You are the ones who have put in the sweat to get here. You have seen blood spilled. We have all shed tears. It's been much more than a game.

"In my past, I've stood in front of teams who have won or lost an important game. I've been fortunate enough to hoist championship trophies. I've consoled players and coaches after heartbreaking losses.

"My friends, I am here today to tell you that I have never been prouder or more honored to be associated with a team than I am with you today. Your performance is nothing short of phenomenal. You went where no one has gone before in the history of this company. You faced adversity and you overcame. You faced defeat and you conquered. You all played to win, and win you did.

Tim Timmons

"The last thing I want to tell you is this. I want you to take a good hard look around you. Look at your peers, your co-workers. I want you to remember not just this day, but I want you to remember this past year. Remember what it took to get here today. Remember the hard work. Remember the sacrifices. Remember what you all gave. That's the price of success. Today is the reward!"

The cheers rose to the rafters. Murphy stood at the front and put his hands up for quiet. When the noise had dimmed a little, Murphy practically screamed into the microphone. "Oh, and before anyone thinks I forgot, besides all the warm and fuzzy stuff, payroll will be handing out bonus checks to every single one of you this afternoon!"

The cheers this time didn't quiet down for a very long time.

A few days later, Walt Smith showed up at Murphy's request. As he got out of his car, he noticed the smell of freshly cut grass. He looked down and saw the bright yellow lines in the lot. He noticed the flagpole was shiny and appeared new. A new door that was crystal clear and swung easily on its hinges had replaced the old door to the plant. When he went inside, Paula Griffin greeted him quickly, politely and professionally. Her workstation was also neat and clean with no fingernail polish to be seen – or smelled. The differences were not lost on the owner.

As Smith waited for Murphy to come up, he was afraid he had an idea about what was coming. Just then, Murph walked through the door, reversing a scene that had only happened a little more than a year ago.

"Coach, I've got to tell you again, you and your folks did a great job," Smith repeated as he shook Murph's hand.

"Thanks, Walt," Murph said as they walked back toward Murph's office. "We had a great group to work with."

"Maybe," Smith said. "But the group was the same for the last three guys to sit in that chair and they couldn't seem to get it done. You're the one who did it."

"Ever thought about who might do it next?" Murph asked.

Smith was afraid that's where this might be going. "No, I was hoping I wouldn't have to worry about that for a while."

"Well, maybe we ought to start thinking about it a little bit."

"Hold on, Coach," Smith said. "You don't want to give this up yet, do you? You've done an amazing job. Let's not jump to any hasty conclusions."

"Walt, I appreciate the opportunity you've given me, I truly do. And financially, you've put Julie and I in a position that we didn't ever dream we'd be in. I think we're going to go to Ireland and look up some long lost relatives. But we need to start thinking about what happens next."

"Coach, let's think this through, OK? You mentioned finances. We can talk about this year."

"Walt, I appreciate it, but here's what I think is a good answer. How about if I stick around a few more months and work with my successor? That way you'll have my replacement in place and the plant won't skip a beat."

"In all fairness to you, Coach, I don't know if I can get a replacement in here that quick. While I would love to do anything you ask me, I don't want to mislead you after all you've done for me and agree to a timetable I can't hit."

"Oh, I don't know Walt," Murph said. "I think you could get someone in pretty short order."

"I don't know, Coach. I've been through this a couple of times. Remember? I've never had much luck in doing this quickly. And this time, it's even more important to get someone who won't let what you've accomplished go for naught. You've come too far."

"I agree," Murph said. "Everyone involved has

worked too hard to let this slide. No one wants to start at square one."

"I don't get it," Smith said. "What's your plan to make this all happen?"

"Promote Bea," Murph said. "She's perfect for the job. Actually, she'll do better than I ever thought about. The plant will excel, the people will be happy and so will you."

"Bea?" Smith said. "I never thought about her for the top job. Are you sure she's ready?"

"Sure?" Murph laughed. "You probably made a mistake by bringing me in instead of promoting her a year ago. Trust me, she's one sharp lady."

"Coach, you know I trust you. You've done more than even I thought possible. If you think Bea's the right choice, I imagine I'll end up agreeing."

Murph smiled.

"Have you already hired her, or do I get to interview her first?" Smith laughed. He raised his hands in surrender before Murphy could react and said, "Just kidding, Coach. If your mind is made up about this, I'll be happy to sit down and talk with Bea. Understand though, I'd rather not lose you. Are you absolutely sure about this? How about taking a couple of days to think it over?"

"Have been, Walt," Murph said. "Julie and I went through the whole thing, pros and cons. I really was ready to retire when I left football. Don't think I'm saying I regret this. I really don't, and I'll always be appreciative of this opportunity. But the timing is right and I'm really ready to kick back and relax. I'll stick around for a little while to make sure the transition goes smoothly, but she's the real thing, Walt. You won't regret this."

The two stood around and talked for a few minutes more. Murphy appreciated an opportunity that he never thought he would have – or want. Smith appreciated a football coach who had gone from charting X's and O's to the CEO position. A year later, it was a move everyone appreciated.

The Author

Mom and Me

Tim Timmons knows a lot about setting and achieving goals. Entering journalism as a reporter and sportswriter for his high school newspaper (where he was named Outstanding Journalism Student as a senior), he climbed the professional ranks from go-fer at his first daily newspaper to become a publisher of a daily paper in his home state of Indiana. He's now the general manager of the South Bend, Ind., newspaper. He and his wife have two teenage daughters, a dog and two cats.

During the writing portion of his career, he won numerous awards. After concentrating on management, Timmons has served on many civic boards and organizations. He also has played and coached tennis and baseball and once set his mind to play for a semi-pro football team when he was in his late 30s. He made the team, despite being a decade and a half older that most of the other players and lived to tell about it. Coach Murphy would call him a "gamer" in any field he decides to pursue.